THE SILVER SPOON

Quick and Easy Italian Recipes

Φ

The deep-rooted love of, and fascination for, food is something that has never changed in Italy. Handed down from generation to generation, recipes are the foundation of Italian family life, but they are worth more than the sum of their parts. They offer practical combinations of ingredients for making tasty, seasonal, and healthy food while also celebrating a way of life that places importance on gathering at the table to break bread together.

The pace of modern times has made eating together even more of a necessity—after all, it is the glue that binds family and society. With *Quick and Easy Italian Recipes*, you can make simple and delicious meals in minutes, and sit down to fabulous and healthy food. Whether it's a Tomato Bruschetta (see page 20) to whet the appetite or Spaghetti Carbonara (see page 78) to satisfy mid-week cravings for comfort food, with some forethought and advance preparation, each of the 100 recipes can be cooked in under 30 minutes. The result? Maximum taste with minimal fuss.

Welcome the flavors of Italy into your home with these classic recipes adapted and brought to you by *The Silver Spoon*, which was first published in Italy in 1950 and in English in 2005, as a collection of some 2,000 recipes gathered from homes and restaurants all over Italy. Italians know a thing or two about joyful living, and when it comes to surrounding yourself with good food and good company, nobody does it better. Buon appetito!

Antipasti

Appetizers

Literally meaning "before the meal," this delightful preamble to lunch and dinner has become a lost art in much of Europe and North America. More than a snack, less than a regular appetizer, these mini-size dishes are traditionally served with a bitter beverage, such as a vermouth, or something with lip-smacking acidity, like a glass of prosecco, both of which work wonders with the saltiness of dishes such as: Carpaccio, paper thin slices of raw beef sprinkled with Parmesan shavings (see page 28); crostini topped with tender chicken livers (see page 14); or Tomato Bruschetta (see page 20). At its most simple, arrange some artichoke hearts from a jar, salami, and a wedge of salty pecorino on a rustic serving plate, for an opener as tantalizing on the eyes as it is on the stomach.

Sage Appetizers

Serves 4
Preparation 10 min, plus standing
Cooking 5 min

— 1 egg
— 30 fresh sage leaves
— ½ cup (1 oz/25 g) fine white bread crumbs
— olive oil, for frying
— salt
— mild provolone cheese, diced

Beat the egg with a pinch of salt in a bowl. Add the sage leaves, making sure that they are immersed, and let stand for 2 minutes. Season the bread crumbs with salt, drain the leaves well, and dip in the bread crumbs to coat.

Heat plenty of olive oil in a skillet or frying pan, add the sage leaves in batches, and cook for 30 seconds on each side, or until golden brown. Drain on paper towels and serve with the provolone.

Buffalo Milk Mozzarella Caprese Salad

Serves 4
Preparation 10 min

— 11 oz/300 g buffalo milk mozzarella cheese
— 3–4 tomatoes, sliced
— basil leaves
— extra virgin olive oil, for drizzling
— salt

Drain the mozzarella and cut into ⅛-inch/ 3-mm slices. Arrange the mozzarella and tomato slices alternately in concentric rings on a large serving plate. Sprinkle with the basil leaves, drizzle with olive oil, and season with salt. Keep in a cool place until ready to serve.

Tuscan Crostini

Serves 4–6
Preparation 20 min
Cooking 20 min

— 2 tablespoons olive oil
— 1 carrot, chopped
— ½ onion, chopped
— 1 celery stalk, chopped
— 6 chicken livers, trimmed and chopped
— scant ½ cup (3½ fl oz/100 ml) dry
   white wine
— 2 egg yolks
— juice of 1 lemon, strained
— 4–6 slices whole wheat (wholemeal)
   bread, lightly toasted
— salt and pepper
— 1 tablespoon capers, drained and
   rinsed, to garnish (optional)

Heat the olive oil in a skillet or frying pan. Add the carrot, onion, and celery and cook over low heat, stirring occasionally, for 5–10 minutes, until softened.

Add the chicken livers to the skillet. Pour in the wine and season with salt and pepper. Cook over medium heat, stirring frequently, for 6–8 minutes until browned all over.

Beat together the egg yolks and lemon juice in a bowl. Pour the egg yolk mixture into the skillet and cook over low heat for 1–2 minutes to thicken slightly. Remove from the heat, let cool, and pulse in a food processor until coarse.

Spread on slices of lightly toasted bread and garnish with the capers, if using. Serve immediately.

Tomato and Anchovy Crostini

Serves 4
Preparation 10 min
Cooking 8–10 min

— 4 slices Tuscan or other rustic bread
— 4 canned anchovy fillets, drained and sliced
— 2 tomatoes, sliced
— 1 pearl (baby) onion, chopped
— 1 tablespoon chopped basil
— extra virgin olive oil, for drizzling
— salt

Preheat the oven to 350°F/180°C/Gas Mark 4 and preheat the broiler (grill) to medium-high heat. Toast the slices of bread under the broiler for 1–2 minutes on each side, or until golden.

Divide the anchovy, slices of tomato, a little chopped onion, and basil between each slice of toast. Drizzle with olive oil and season with salt. Put the toasts on a baking sheet and heat in the oven for 4–5 minutes, then serve.

Sausage Crostini

Serves 4–6
Preparation 10 min
Cooking 15 min

— 3 Italian sausages, casings removed
— 5 oz/150 g stracchino cheese, such as
  taleggio or robiola, chopped
— 1 tablespoon fennel seeds
— 4–6 slices country-style (farmhouse)
  bread
— salt

Preheat the oven to 350°F/180°C/Gas Mark 4. Crumble the sausages into a bowl and mix in the cheese and fennel seeds. Season with salt to taste and stir well. Spread the mixture on the slices of bread, place on a baking sheet, and bake for 15 minutes, or until crisp and golden. Arrange on a plate and serve immediately while still hot.

Tomato Bruschetta

Serves 4
Preparation 15 min
Cooking 5 min

— 8 slices country-style (farmhouse)
  bread
— 1 clove garlic
— 6–8 ripe plum tomatoes, diced
— extra virgin olive oil, for drizzling
— salt and pepper

Preheat the broiler (grill). Toast the slices of bread under the broiler for 1–2 minutes on each side, or until golden. Rub them with garlic while they are still hot and put back under the broiler for a moment. Arrange the tomatoes on the toasts. Season with salt and pepper and drizzle with olive oil.

Panzanella

Serves 4
Preparation 15 min

— 4 firm red tomatoes
— 8 slices stale, rustic white bread,
   crusts removed
— 8 basil leaves, torn
— extra virgin olive oil, for drizzling
— salt and pepper

Blanch the tomatoes in a heatproof bowl of boiling water for a few seconds, then peel and cut into wedges.

Tear the bread into pieces and soak in a bowl of cold water for 1–2 minutes, then squeeze out and put into a salad bowl. Season with salt and pepper, sprinkle with the basil, and drizzle generously with oil.

Toss the bread with 2 forks so that it crumbles, then add the tomatoes.

Belgian Endive with Crab

Serves 4
Preparation 15 min

— 2–3 heads Belgian endive (chicory)
— 1 cup (8 fl oz/250 ml) Mayonnaise
  (see page 226) or store-bought
— 9 oz/250 g canned or fresh crabmeat,
  drained
— 2 tablespoons heavy (double) cream
— 2 tablespoons ketchup
— ½ teaspoon Worcestershire sauce
— brandy, for drizzling (optional)
— salt and pepper

Separate the Belgian endive (chicory) into individual leaves and arrange on a serving dish.

Combine the mayonnaise and crabmeat in a bowl, gently stir in the cream, ketchup, and Worcestershire sauce, and drizzle with the brandy, if using. Mix gently.

Put 1 tablespoon of the mixture into the concave part of each Belgian endive leaf, season to taste, and serve.

Rolled Bell Peppers

Serves 4
Preparation 25 min
Cooking 10 min

— 4 large red or green bell peppers
— 11 oz/300 g canned tuna in oil,
   drained
— 10 pitted black olives, coarsely
   chopped
— 1 tomato, peeled, seeded, and coarsely
   chopped
— 1 fresh red chile, seeded and coarsely
   chopped
— 12 fresh basil leaves
— 3–4 tablespoons lemon juice, strained
— 1 tablespoon olive oil
— salt and pepper

Put the bell peppers on a baking sheet under a preheated broiler (grill). Broil (grill), turning frequently, for 10 minutes, or until charred and blackened. Transfer to a plastic bag, tie the top, and let cool.

Peel off the bell pepper skins, rinse gently under cold running water, and pat dry. Halve and seed the bell peppers, then cut the flesh into two or three large slices.

Put the tuna, olives, tomato, chile, and basil into a food processor and process to a puree. Add enough lemon juice to make a soft mixture, add the olive oil, season to taste, and mix well.

Spread each slice of bell pepper with the tuna sauce and roll up. Keep in a cool place before serving.

Carpaccio

Serves 4
Preparation 15 min

— 12 oz/350 g lean beef, such as sirloin, thinly sliced
— 4 radishes, thinly sliced (optional)
— juice of 1 lemon, strained
— extra virgin olive oil, for drizzling
— 4–5 white peppercorns, crushed
— 3½ oz/100 g Grana Padano cheese, shaved into flakes
— salt

Spread out the slices of meat on a serving plate, slightly overlapping, and arrange the radish slices on top, if using.

In a small bowl, whisk together the lemon juice, a drizzle of oil, white peppercorns, and a pinch of salt. Pour the dressing over the beef, sprinkle with the cheese, and serve.

First Courses

In Italy, pasta tends to come in smaller portions, but there's no reason you can't serve it as a quick midweek dinner. If going all out for a full-course Italian meal, remember the point of "primi" is to satisfy the appetite after the taster of the "antipasti," but not to overstuff. You would pair it with something crisp and refreshing, such as a pinot grigio. There are hundreds of different sauces and almost as many different pasta shapes designed to suit any menu, ranging from something as basic as Tagliatelle with Lemon (see page 64), or Penne alla Vodka (see page 76), to a crowd-pleasing weekend Lasagne Bolognese made with a traditional ragu (see page 80).

Pasta with Tomato Sauce

Serves 4
Preparation 15 min
Cooking 15 min

— 6 plum tomatoes
— 4 tablespoons olive oil
— 2 cloves garlic, chopped
— 1 parsley sprig
— 12 oz/350 g long or short pasta, such
   as spaghetti, fettuccine, or fusilli
— 10 basil leaves, torn
— salt

Blanch the tomatoes in a heatproof bowl of boiling water for a few seconds, then peel, seed, and dice. Put into a small saucepan and add the olive oil, garlic, parsley, and a pinch of salt. Cook, uncovered, over medium heat for 10 minutes. If you like a stronger flavor, thicken the sauce over high heat for the last 5 minutes of the cooking time, making sure it does not stick to the pan.

Meanwhile, cook the pasta in a large saucepan of salted, boiling water until al dente and drain.

Remove and discard the parsley from the sauce. Stir in the torn basil, taste, and add more salt, if necessary. Pour the sauce directly over the drained pasta while still hot.

First Courses

Pizza-Style Fusilli

Serves 4
Preparation 20 min
Cooking 20 min

— butter, for greasing
— 4 ripe tomatoes, chopped
— 1 tablespoon olive oil, plus extra
  for drizzling
— 12 oz/350 g fusilli or other short pasta
— pinch of dried oregano
— 1 tablespoon chopped basil
— ½ cup (1½ oz/40 g) grated Parmesan
  cheese
— 3½ oz/100 g mozzarella cheese,
  diced
— salt

Preheat the oven to 350°F/180°C/Gas Mark 4 and grease an ovenproof dish with butter.

Process the tomatoes to a puree in a food processor or blender. Heat the oil in a small saucepan. Add the pureed tomatoes and cook over low heat, stirring occasionally, for 10 minutes, or until thickened.

Meanwhile, cook the pasta in a large saucepan of salted, boiling water until al dente. Drain, and return to the pan. Stir the oregano and basil into the tomato sauce and pour it over the pasta. Sprinkle with the Parmesan and toss well to mix.

Spoon the mixture into the prepared dish, top with the diced mozzarella, and drizzle with oil. Bake for 10 minutes, or until the mozzarella starts to melt. Serve immediately straight from the dish.

First Courses

Penne Arrabbiata

Serves 4
Preparation 10 min
Cooking 20 min

— 5 tablespoons olive oil
— 2 cloves garlic
— 1–2 fresh red chiles, according to
taste, seeded and chopped
— 1 (14½-oz/400-g) can diced or
chopped tomatoes, drained
— 12 oz/350 g penne
— 1 tablespoon chopped flat-leaf parsley
— salt

Heat the oil in a skillet or frying pan, add the garlic and chile, and cook for 5 minutes, or until the garlic browns. Remove the garlic from the skillet and add the tomatoes, season with salt, and cook for about 15 minutes.

Meanwhile, cook the penne in a large saucepan of salted, boiling water until al dente, then drain and add to the skillet. Toss over high heat for a few minutes, then transfer to a warm serving dish and sprinkle with the parsley.

Conchiglie with Mozzarella

Serves 4
Preparation 10 min
Cooking 10 min

— 5 plum tomatoes, peeled
  and diced
— 7 oz/200 g diced mozzarella cheese
— 10 basil leaves, torn
— 1 tablespoon capers, drained and
  rinsed
— ⅔ cup (5 fl oz/150 ml) extra virgin
  olive oil
— 12 oz/350 g conchiglie (shell pasta)
— salt and pepper

Put the tomatoes, mozzarella, basil, capers, and olive oil into a serving dish.

Cook the pasta in a large saucepan of salted, boiling water until al dente. Drain and immediately add to the mixture in the dish so that the mozzarella melts slightly. Season with salt and pepper, toss well and serve.

Pappardelle with Cauliflower and Gorgonzola

Serves 4
Preparation 10 min
Cooking 25 min

— 1½ cups (7 oz/200 g) cauliflower
  florets
— 1½ tablespoons (¾ oz/20 g) butter
— 5 oz/150 g Gorgonzola cheese, diced
— 3–4 tablespoons milk (optional)
— 3 tablespoons olive oil
— 1 clove garlic
— 1 tablespoon chopped thyme
— 10 oz/275 g fresh pappardelle
— ⅓ cup (1 oz/25 g) grated Parmesan
  cheese
— salt and pepper

Parboil the cauliflower in a medium saucepan of salted, boiling water for 5 minutes, then remove, using a slotted spoon, reserving the cooking water.

Melt the butter with the Gorgonzola in a small saucepan over low heat, stirring continuously and adding a little milk, if necessary. Do not let the mixture boil. Remove the pan from the heat.

Heat the oil in a large skillet or frying pan. Add the garlic and cook over low heat, stirring frequently, for a few minutes until lightly browned. Remove the garlic and discard. Add the cauliflower to the skillet and cook, stirring occasionally, for 5 minutes. Sprinkle with the thyme and season with salt and pepper.

Cook the pappardelle in the reserved cooking water, adding more boiling water, if necessary, for 2–3 minutes until al dente. Drain and add to the skillet with the cauliflower. Stir in the Gorgonzola mixture, remove from the heat, and serve sprinkled with the grated Parmesan.

Orecchiette with Broccoli

Serves 4
Preparation 15 min
Cooking 15 min

— 7 cups (1 lb 5 oz/600 g) broccoli
  florets
— 2 tablespoons olive oil
— 1 clove garlic, chopped
— 1 fresh chile, seeded and chopped
— 11 oz/300 g orecchiette
— salt
— Parmesan or pecorino cheese,
  freshly grated, to serve

Cook the broccoli in a medium saucepan of salted, boiling water for 2–3 minutes, then drain. Heat the olive oil in a large saucepan, add the garlic and chile, and cook for 2–3 minutes. Add the broccoli and cook over low heat for 1–2 minutes until heated through.

Meanwhile, cook the orecchiette in a large saucepan of salted, boiling water until al dente, drain, and toss with the broccoli. Serve with the Parmesan or pecorino.

Spring Linguine

Serves 4
Preparation 10 min
Cooking 15 min

— 4 tablespoons (2 oz/50 g) butter
— 2 tablespoons olive oil
— 2 scallions (spring onions), chopped
— 2⅔ cups (14 oz/400 g) shelled or frozen peas
— 14 oz/400 g asparagus, trimmed and cut diagonally
— 12 oz/350 g linguine
— ⅔ cup (2 oz/50 g) grated Parmesan cheese
— salt and pepper

Melt half the butter with the oil in a saute pan. Add the scallions (spring onions) and cook over low heat for 3–5 minutes, or until soft and translucent. Add the peas and asparagus, season with salt and pepper, stir in ⅔ cup (5 fl oz/ 150 ml) hot water, and simmer for 5 minutes.

Meanwhile, cook the linguine in a large saucepan of salted, boiling water until al dente. Drain, transfer to the pan with the vegetables, and mix. Stir in the remaining butter and the Parmesan and serve immediately.

First Courses

Conchiglie with Spinach

Serves 4
Preparation 10 min
Cooking 15 min

— 4 tablespoons (2 oz/50 g) butter
— 1 shallot, chopped
— 6 cups (14 oz/400 g) spinach, chopped
— 12 oz/350 g conchiglie (shell pasta)
— 1 egg or 4 tablespoons light (single)
  cream
— scant ½ cup (3½ oz/100 g) ricotta
  cheese
— salt and pepper

Melt the butter in a large saucepan. Add the shallot and cook over low heat, stirring occasionally, for 5 minutes. Add the spinach and stir well, then season with salt, cover, and cook for a few minutes until wilted. Be careful to remove the pan from the heat before the mixture dries out.

Meanwhile, cook the pasta in a large saucepan of salted, boiling water until al dente.

Put the egg (or cream, if using) and ricotta into a serving dish, season well with salt and pepper, and beat until smooth and combined.

Drain the pasta and stir the pasta into the ricotta mixture. Add the spinach mixture, toss lightly, and serve immediately.

Linguine with Genoese Pesto

Serves 4
Preparation 15 min
Cooking 10 min

— 12 oz/350 g linguine
— 2 potatoes, cut into thin sticks
— ⅓ cup (2 oz/50 g) green beans

For the pesto
— 25 basil leaves
— 2 cloves garlic, chopped
— 5 tablespoons extra virgin olive oil
— ⅓ cup (1 oz/25 g) freshly grated
  pecorino cheese
— ⅓ cup (1 oz/25 g) freshly grated
  Parmesan cheese
— salt

To make the pesto, put the basil, garlic, olive oil, and a pinch of salt into a food processor and process briefly at medium speed. Add both cheeses and process again until blended.

Cook the linguine, potatoes, and beans together in a large saucepan of salted, boiling water until al dente, then drain. Toss with the pesto and serve.

Tortiglioni with Mushroom and Eggplant

Serves 4
Preparation 10 min
Cooking 20 min

— 2 tablespoons olive oil
— 1 onion, thinly sliced
— 1 clove garlic
— 2¾ cups (7 oz/200 g) chopped mushrooms
— 1 eggplant (aubergine), cut into ½-inch/1-cm dice
— scant ½ cup (3½ fl oz/100 ml) heavy (double) cream
— 12 oz/350 g tortiglioni or penne
— ½ cup (1½ oz/40 g) grated Parmesan cheese
— salt and pepper

Bring a large saucepan of salted water to a boil. Heat the oil in a large skillet or frying pan, add the onion and garlic, and cook over low heat for 5 minutes until softened. Remove and discard the garlic, add the mushrooms and eggplant (aubergine) to the skillet, and cook over medium–high heat for 5 minutes, stirring frequently, until light golden brown. Stir in the cream, season with salt and pepper, cover, and cook over low heat for another 10 minutes.

Meanwhile, cook the tortiglioni in the pan of salted, boiling water until al dente, then drain, add to the skillet of sauce, and cook for 1 minute. Transfer to a warm serving dish and sprinkle with the Parmesan.

Rigatoni with Garbanzo Bean Sauce

Serves 4
Preparation 15 min
Cooking 15 min

— 1½ cups (9 oz/250 g) cooked or canned garbanzo beans (chickpeas), drained
— 4 tablespoons olive oil
— 1 clove garlic
— 1 sprig rosemary, finely chopped, plus extra to garnish (optional)
— 12 oz/350 g rigatoni
— salt and pepper
— 1 sprig flat-leaf parsley, finely chopped, to garnish (optional)
— Parmesan cheese, freshly grated, to serve (optional)

Put half of the garbanzo beans (chickpeas) and 1 tablespoon of the oil into a food processor or blender and process to a puree.

Heat the remaining oil in a saucepan. Add the garlic and cook over low heat, stirring frequently, for a few minutes until lightly browned. Remove the garlic and discard. Add the pureed garbanzo beans and the whole garbanzo beans to the pan, sprinkle with the rosemary, and season well with salt and pepper. Cook over low heat, stirring frequently, for 10 minutes.

Meanwhile, cook the rigatoni in a large saucepan of salted, boiling water until al dente. Drain, reserving ¼ cup (2 fl oz/60 ml) of the cooking water. Transfer the rigatoni to a warm serving dish. Loosen the garbanzo bean sauce with the reserved cooking water, if necessary, and pour over the pasta. Garnish with rosemary sprigs or parsley, and Parmesan cheese, if using, and serve immediately.

Taglierini with Shallots

Serves 4
Preparation 10 min
Cooking 25–30 min

— 4 tablespoons (2 oz/50 g) butter
— 2 shallots, thinly sliced
— 10 oz/275 g fresh taglierini or
  tagliatelle
— ⅔ cup (2 oz/50 g) grated Gruyère
  cheese
— generous ⅓ cup (1¼ oz/30 g) grated
  Parmesan cheese
— salt

Melt the butter in a skillet or frying pan. Add the shallots and cook over low heat, stirring occasionally, for 25–30 minutes until golden brown and caramelized.

Meanwhile, cook the taglierini in a large saucepan of salted, boiling water for 2–3 minutes until al dente. Drain and immediately add the pasta to the hot skillet. Toss well, transfer to a warm serving dish, sprinkle with the Gruyère and Parmesan, and serve immediately.

Penne with Black Olives

Serves 4
Preparation 15 min
Cooking 15 min

— 1¼ cups (5 oz/150 g) pitted black
  olives, sliced
— ¾ cup (6 fl oz/175 ml) heavy (double)
  cream
— 12 oz/350 g penne
— ⅓ cup (1 oz/25 g) grated Parmesan
  cheese
— salt

Put the olives and cream into a medium saucepan
and cook over low heat for about 15 minutes.

Meanwhile, cook the penne in a large saucepan
of salted, boiling water until al dente, then drain.
Add the pasta and Parmesan to the sauce, mix
well and serve.

Fettuccine with Walnut Sauce

Serves 4
Preparation 20 min, plus standing
Cooking 10 min

— 2¼ cups (9 oz/250 g) shelled walnuts
— 4 tablespoons olive oil
— 2 tablespoons heavy (double) cream
— 12 oz/350 g fettuccine
— salt and white pepper

Put the walnuts into a heatproof bowl and pour in boiling water to cover. Let stand for 3 minutes, then drain. When the nuts are cool enough to handle, rub off the skins. Rinse with cold water to wash away the skins.

Pat dry with paper towels and put the nuts into a food processor and process until coarsely chopped. Transfer to a bowl with the olive oil and cream. Season with salt and white pepper and mix to an even consistency.

Cook the fettuccine in a large saucepan of salted, boiling water until al dente, then drain and toss the walnut mixture through.

Conchiglie with Gorgonzola and Pistachios

Serves 4
Preparation 15 min, plus standing
Cooking 15 min

— ½ cup (2 oz/50 g) pistachios
— 3½ oz/100 g strong Gorgonzola, diced
— ¾ cup (6 fl oz/175 ml) heavy (double) cream
— 11 oz/300 g conchiglie (shell pasta)
— ½ cup (1½ oz/40 g) grated Parmesan cheese
— salt

Put the pistachios into a small heatproof bowl and pour in boiling water to cover. Let stand for 3 minutes and drain. When cool enough to handle, rub off the skins with your fingers. Chop the pistachios and set aside.

Put the Gorgonzola and cream into a small saucepan and heat gently for about 10 minutes, stirring constantly until the cheese has melted and the sauce is completely smooth, then remove from the heat.

Meanwhile, cook the pasta in a large saucepan of salted, boiling water until al dente. Drain, transfer to a warm serving dish, and toss with the melted Gorgonzola mixture, chopped pistachios, and Parmesan. Serve immediately.

Macaroni au Gratin

Serves 4
Preparation 10 min
Cooking 25–30 min

— 2 tablespoons (1 oz/20 g) butter, plus extra for greasing
— scant 2 cups (15 fl oz/450 ml) Béchamel Sauce (see page 226) or store-bought
— ⅔ cup (2 oz/50 g) freshly grated Parmesan cheese
— 2 egg yolks
— 12 oz/350 g macaroni
— salt

Preheat the oven to 425°F/220°C/Gas Mark 7. Grease an ovenproof baking dish with butter.

Combine the béchamel sauce, Parmesan, butter, and egg yolks in a bowl.

Cook the macaroni in a large saucepan of salted, boiling water until al dente, then drain and pour into a bowl. Gently stir in half the béchamel sauce mixture and put the pasta in the prepared dish, then spoon the remaining béchamel sauce mixture on top. Bake in the oven for 15–20 minutes, until golden brown.

Tagliatelle with Lemon

Serves 4
Preparation 10 min
Cooking 15 min

— 3 unwaxed lemons
— 4 tablespoons (2 oz/50 g) butter
— 4 tablespoons light (single) cream
— 10 oz/275 g fresh tagliatelle
— salt
— finely grated Parmesan cheese,
   to serve

Grate the zest of 2 of the lemons. Peel the remaining lemon, removing all traces of pith from the zest and cut it into thin strips.

Melt the butter in a skillet or frying pan. When it foams, add the grated lemon zest and cook, stirring occasionally, for a few minutes, then stir in the cream and season with salt. Do not let the mixture boil.

Meanwhile, cook the tagliatelle in a large saucepan of salted, boiling water for 2–3 minutes until al dente. Drain, transfer to the skillet with the sauce, and toss gently. Transfer to a serving dish, sprinkle with plenty of Parmesan, and garnish with the strips of lemon rind.

Spaghetti with Garlic and Chili Oil

Serves 4
Preparation 10 min
Cooking 10 min

— 12 oz/350 g spaghetti
— 5 tablespoons olive oil
— 2 cloves garlic, thinly sliced
— 1 fresh chile, seeded and chopped
— 1 sprig flat-leaf parsley, chopped
— salt

Cook the spaghetti in a large saucepan of salted, boiling water until al dente, then drain, reserving ½ cup (4 fl oz/120 ml) of the cooking water.

Meanwhile, heat the oil in a small saucepan, add the garlic and chile, and cook over low heat for 5 minutes, or until the garlic is softened and golden brown. Season lightly with salt, remove the pan from the heat, and add the parsley.

Toss the spaghetti with the garlic and chili oil, add some of the reserved cooking water to loosen, if necessary, and serve.

Spaghettini with Clams

Serves 4
Preparation 10 min
Cooking 20 min

— 2¼ lb/1 kg small clams, cleaned
— scant 1 cup (7 fl oz/200 ml) olive oil
— 2 cloves garlic, peeled
— 2 tablespoons chopped flat-leaf parsley
— 11½ oz/320 g spaghettini
— salt and pepper

Discard any clams with damaged shells or that do not shut immediately when sharply tapped.

Heat the oil with the garlic cloves in a large saucepan. When they are beginning to brown, remove and discard the garlic cloves. Add the clams to the pan, cover, and cook, occasionally shaking the pan, for 3–4 minutes, until the shells have opened.

Remove the pan from the heat and lift out the clams with a slotted spoon and put them into a shallow dish. Discard any that remain shut. Remove the clams from their shells. Strain any juices left behind in the dish into the pan, then add the clams and parsley and season with salt and pepper.

Cook the spaghettini in a large saucepan of salted, boiling water until al dente. Drain, add to the pan with the clams, toss over high heat, and serve.

Note: For a variation on this clam sauce, you can add a few chopped tomatoes.

Tagliatelle with Salmon

Serves 4
Preparation 5 min
Cooking 15 min

— 4 tablespoons (2 oz/50 g) butter
— 3½ oz/100 g smoked salmon, chopped
— juice of ½ lemon, strained
— scant ½ cup (3½ fl oz/100 ml) heavy
  (double) cream
— 10 oz/275 g tagliatelle
— salt and pepper

Melt the butter in a medium skillet or frying pan, add the salmon, stir, and sprinkle with the lemon juice. Cook for a few minutes, then add the cream and season to taste. Cook over low heat for 5 minutes.

Cook the tagliatelle in a large saucepan of salted, boiling water until al dente, drain, add to the skillet with the sauce, and cook for a few minutes. Toss gently and serve immediately.

Fettuccine with Chicken and Almonds

Serves 4
Preparation 20 min
Cooking 25 min

— 2 tablespoons (1 oz/25 g) butter
— 1 shallot, chopped
— 2 (5 oz/150 g) skinless boneless
  chicken breasts, chopped
— scant ½ cup (3½ fl oz/100 ml) dry
  white wine
— ⅓ cup (1½ oz/40 g) almonds, chopped
— scant 1 cup (7 fl oz/200 ml) heavy
  (double) cream
— 10 oz/275 g fettuccine
— ⅓ cup (1 oz/25 g) grated Parmesan
  cheese
— salt and pepper

Melt the butter in a skillet or frying pan. Add the shallot and cook over low heat, stirring occasionally, for 5 minutes. Add the chicken, stir well, and cook for 5 minutes. Pour in the wine and cook for 2 minutes, then add the almonds and stir in the cream. Simmer over low heat, stirring occasionally, for about 10 minutes, then season with salt and pepper.

Meanwhile, cook the fettuccine in a large saucepan of salted, boiling water until al dente. Drain, transfer to a warm serving dish, pour the chicken sauce over it, and sprinkle with the Parmesan. Serve immediately.

Linguine with Broccoli and Pancetta

Serves 4
Preparation 15 min
Cooking 25 min

— 2 tablespoons olive oil
— 4 oz/120 g diced pancetta
  or thick-cut bacon
— 1 clove garlic, finely chopped
— 7 cups (1 lb 5 oz/600 g) broccoli
  florets
— 1 tablespoon tomato paste (purée)
— ⅔ cup (5 fl oz/150 ml) vegetable
  broth (stock)
— 12 oz/350 g linguine
— ½ cup (1½ oz/40 g) grated
  Parmesan cheese
— salt

Heat the oil in large skillet or frying pan. Add the pancetta and cook over medium–low heat, stirring occasionally, for 4–5 minutes. Stir in the garlic and half the broccoli and cook, stirring occasionally, for 5 minutes. Stir in the tomato paste (purée) and broth (stock), lower the heat, and simmer for 10 minutes, until the broccoli is tender but still firm.

Meanwhile, cook the pasta with the remaining broccoli in a large saucepan of salted, boiling water until al dente. Drain, add to the skillet with the sauce, and toss over the heat for a few minutes. Transfer to a warm serving dish, sprinkle with the Parmesan, and serve immediately.

First Courses

Penne alla Vodka

Serves 4
Preparation 5 min
Cooking 20 min

— 4 tablespoons (2 oz/50 g) butter
— 1 (2 oz/50 g) slice cooked ham
— 2 tablespoons tomato paste (purée)
— 1 tablespoon chopped flat-leaf parsley
— 5 tablespoons heavy (double) cream
— 3 tablespoons vodka
— 12 oz/350 g penne
— salt and pepper

Melt the butter in a small saucepan over low–medium heat, add the ham, tomato paste (purée), and parsley, season with salt and pepper, and cook, stirring occasionally, for about 10 minutes. Stir in the cream and vodka and cook until the vodka has evaporated.

Meanwhile, cook the penne in a large saucepan of salted, boiling water until al dente, then drain, and transfer to a warm serving dish. Pour the sauce over the pasta.

Spaghetti Carbonara

Serves 4
Preparation 15 min
Cooking 20 min

— 2 tablespoons (1 oz/25 g) butter
— 3½ oz/100 g pancetta or thick-cut bacon, diced
— 1 clove garlic
— 12 oz/350 g spaghetti
— 2 eggs, beaten
— ½ cup (1½ oz/40 g) freshly grated Parmesan cheese
— ½ cup (1½ oz/40 g) freshly grated pecorino cheese
— salt and pepper

Melt the butter in a large saucepan, add the pancetta and garlic, and cook for 5 minutes, or until the garlic turns brown. Remove and discard the garlic. Continue to cook the pancetta for another 5 minutes.

Meanwhile, cook the spaghetti in a large saucepan of salted, boiling water until al dente, then drain and add to the pancetta.

Remove the pan from the heat, pour in the eggs, add half the Parmesan and half the pecorino, and season with pepper. Mix well so that the egg coats the pasta. Add the remaining cheese, mix again, and serve.

Lasagne Bolognese

Serves 4
Preparation 15 min
Cooking 30 min

— 2 tablespoons (1 oz/25 g) butter,
  plus extra for greasing
— 8–12 oven-ready lasagne noodles
  (sheets)
— 1 quantity Ragu (see page 227)
— 1 quantity Béchamel Sauce (see
  page 226) or store-bought
— scant 1 cup (2½ oz/65 g) freshly
  grated Parmesan cheese

Preheat the oven to 400°F/200°C/Gas Mark 6. Grease a deep-sided ovenproof baking dish with butter. Arrange a layer of lasagna noodles (sheets) to cover the bottom of the prepared dish, spoon over one third of the ragu to cover the noodles, then one quarter of the béchamel sauce to cover the ragu, sprinkle with one quarter of the Parmesan, and dot with one third of the butter.

Repeat the alternate layers until all the ingredients have been used, ending with a layer of béchamel sauce and Parmesan. Bake in the oven for 30 minutes.

Asparagus Risotto

Serves 4–6
Preparation 10 min
Cooking 30 min

— 6¼ cups (2½ pints/1.5 liters) vegetable broth (stock)
— 5 tablespoons (2½ oz/65 g) butter
— 3 tablespoons olive oil
— 1 lb 2 oz/500 g asparagus, spears trimmed, tips reserved, and stems chopped
— ½ onion, chopped
— 2 cups (12 oz/350 g) risotto rice
— Parmesan cheese, freshly grated, to serve

Bring the broth (stock) to a boil in a large saucepan and adjust the heat to keep it at a boil.

Melt 3 tablespoons of the butter and the oil in a large saucepan, add the asparagus spears and onion, and cook over low heat, stirring occasionally, for 5 minutes until softened. Remove the spears and set aside.

Add the rice to the butter and oil and cook, stirring, for 1–2 minutes, until the grains are coated in fat, then add the chopped asparagus stems. Increase the heat, add a ladleful of the hot broth and cook, stirring, until it has been absorbed. Continue adding the broth, a ladleful at a time, stirring continuously until each addition has been absorbed before adding the next, This will take 15–20 minutes. When half of the broth has been added, add the asparagus tips. When the rice is tender, stir in the remaining butter and the asparagus spears. Serve with Parmesan.

First Courses

Mushroom Risotto

Serves 4–6
Preparation 10 min
Cooking 30 min

— 4¼ cups (1¾ pints/1 liter) hot
   vegetable broth (stock)
— 6 tablespoons (3 oz/80 g) butter
— 1 tablespoon olive oil
— 1 onion, finely chopped
— 1⅔ cups (11½ oz/320 g) risotto rice
— 14 oz/400 g mixed mushrooms,
   such as cremini (chestnut) and oyster,
   thinly sliced
— salt and pepper

Bring the broth (stock) to a boil in a large
saucepan and adjust the heat to keep it at a boil.

Melt 2 tablespoons of the butter with 1 tablespoon
of the oil in a large saucepan, add the onion, and
cook over low heat, stirring occasionally, for
5 minutes until softened. Add the rice to the
onion and cook, stirring, for 1–2 minutes, until
the grains are coated in fat. Increase the heat,
add a ladleful of the hot broth, and cook, stirring,
until it has been absorbed. Continue adding the
broth, a ladleful at a time, stirring continuously
until each addition has been absorbed before
adding the next. This will take 15–20 minutes.

Meanwhile, melt 2 tablespoons of the butter in
a large skillet or frying pan, add the mushrooms,
season with salt and pepper, cover, and cook over
low heat.

When all of the stock has been added, gently
stir in the mushrooms and juices into the risotto.
Remove from the heat, gently stir in the remaining
butter, season to taste, and transfer to a warm
serving dish. Serve immediately.

Milanese Risotto

Serves 4–6
Preparation 10 min
Cooking 30 min, plus standing

— about 6¼ cups (2½ pints/1.5 liters)
  meat broth (stock)
— 6 tablespoons (3 oz/80 g) butter
— ¾ oz/20 g beef bone marrow, removed
  from the bone and chopped (optional)
— 1 small onion, chopped
— 2 cups (12 oz/350 g) risotto rice
— ½ cup (4 fl oz/120 ml) white wine
  (optional)
— ½ teaspoon saffron threads
— 1 cup (3 oz/80 g) freshly grated
  Parmesan cheese
— salt and pepper

Bring the broth (stock) to a boil in a large saucepan and adjust the heat to keep it at a boil.

In a large saucepan, heat 4 tablespoons of the butter and the bone marrow, if using. Add the onion and cook over low heat, stirring occasionally, for 5 minutes until softened. Add the rice to the onion and cook, stirring, for 1–2 minutes, until the grains are coated in butter. Increase the heat. If using, pour in the wine and cook, stirring, until evaporated. Add a ladleful of the hot broth and cook, stirring, until it has been absorbed. Continue adding the broth, a ladleful at a time, stirring continuously until each addition has been absorbed before adding the next. This will take 15–20 minutes.

In the meantime, boil some water. Put the saffron in a small heatproof bowl and add 2 tablespoons of boiling water. Let stand for 10 minutes.

Before adding the final ladleful of broth to the rice, stir in the saffron liquid. When the rice is tender, season to taste. Remove the pan from the heat and stir in the remaining butter and the Parmesan. Cover and let stand for 5 minutes, then serve.

First Courses

Summer Rice Salad

Serves 4
Preparation 10 min
Cooking 20 min

— 1½ cups (11 oz/300 g) instant (easy-
 cook) rice
— 9 oz/250 g canned tuna in oil, drained
 and flaked
— 7 oz/200 g Gruyère cheese, diced
— 4 tomatoes, seeded and diced
— 2 tablespoons capers, drained and
 rinsed
— 3 tablespoons extra virgin olive oil
— juice of 1 lemon, strained
— 8 pickled pearl (silverskin) onions
— 8 baby artichoke hearts or quarters
 in oil, drained
— salt and pepper

Cook the rice in a medium saucepan of salted, boiling water until tender, then drain, rinse under cold running water, and drain again.

Meanwhile, put the tuna, cheese, tomatoes, and capers into a salad bowl. Add the rice and mix well so that it soaks up the flavors.

Whisk together the olive oil and lemon juice in a small bowl, then pour the dressing over the salad and toss. Finally, mix in the onions and artichokes and season to taste. Store in a cool place, but not in the refrigerator, until ready to serve.

Watercress Soup

Serves 4
Preparation 15 min
Cooking 30 min

— 2 tablespoons (1 oz/25 g) butter
— 2 leeks, white part only, thinly sliced
— 3 potatoes, diced
— 4¼ cups (1¾ pints/1 liter) vegetable broth (stock)
— 9 oz/250 g chopped watercress or young spinach leaves
— pinch of freshly grated nutmeg
— ⅔ cup (5 fl oz/150 ml) heavy (double) cream
— salt and pepper
— buttered croutons, to serve

Melt the butter in a large saucepan, add the leeks, and cook over low heat, stirring occasionally, for 5 minutes, until softened. Add the potatoes, pour in the broth (stock), and cook over low heat for 10 minutes. Add the watercress and nutmeg, season with salt and pepper, and cook for another 10 minutes.

Transfer to a food processor and process until smooth, in batches, if necessary. Pour the mixture back into the pan, stir in the cream, and reheat briefly. Serve with croutons.

Cream of Carrot Soup

Serves 6
Preparation 30 min
Cooking 30 min

— 4⅓ cups (1¾ lb/800 g) chopped
  carrots
— 1 clove garlic
— 2¼ cups (18 fl oz/500 ml) milk
— 1¾ cups (14 fl oz/400 ml) meat broth
  (stock)
— ⅓ cup (1½ oz/40 g) finely grated
  fontina cheese
— pinch of freshly grated nutmeg
— salt and pepper

Put the carrots and garlic into a Dutch oven or casserole, pour in just enough water to cover, and add a pinch of salt. Bring to a boil over medium heat and cook for 15 minutes, or until almost all the liquid is absorbed.

Transfer to a food processor and process to a puree, in batches, if necessary. Pour the mixture back into the Dutch oven. Stir the milk into the carrot puree along with the broth (stock), and mix well. Cook for 10 minutes, or until fairly thick. In the meantime, preheat the broiler (grill).

Season to taste and sprinkle with the fontina, nutmeg, and a pinch of pepper. Put the Dutch oven under the broiler to melt the cheese, and serve immediately.

Bread Soup with Tomato

Serves 4
Preparation 5 min
Cooking 30 min

— 1 tablespoon olive oil
— 1 clove garlic, chopped
— 2 celery stalks, thinly sliced
— 2 (7 oz/400 g) cans chopped tomatoes
— 4 slices day-old country-style bread, cubed
— 6 basil leaves, chopped
— ⅓ cup freshly grated Parmesan cheese
— salt and pepper

Put the oil, garlic, celery, into a large saucepan, season well, and fry for 3–5 minutes until the celery is softened and translucent.

Add the tomatoes and 1⅔ cups (14 fl oz/400 ml) warm water. Lower the heat and simmer for 25 minutes.

Put a slice of bread in the bottom of each bowl and pour the soup over the bread. Sprinkle with the basil and Parmesan, and serve.

Lettuce and Mint Soup

Serves 4
Preparation 10 min
Cooking 20 min

— 2 tablespoons (1 oz/25 g) butter
— 1 onion, thinly sliced into rings
— 1 lettuce, shredded
— 4¼ cups (1¾ pints/1 liter) vegetable
  broth (stock)
— 15 mint leaves
— 2 tablespoons heavy (double) cream
— salt and pepper
— croutons, to serve

Melt the butter in a Dutch oven or casserole.
Add the onion and cook over low heat, stirring
occasionally, for 5 minutes, until softened and
translucent. Add the lettuce and cook for
3–4 minutes, then pour in the stock and season
with salt and pepper.

Increase the heat to medium and bring to a boil,
then reduce the heat and simmer for 5 minutes.
Stir in the mint leaves and remove the Dutch oven
from the heat.

Transfer to a food processor and process until
smooth, in batches, if necessary. Pour the mixture
back into the Dutch oven, stir in the cream, and
reheat gently but do not let boil. Ladle into warm
soup bowls and serve with croutons.

Second Courses

"Secondi" is the main event. Even in today's less affluent Italy, there is still a great deal of importance placed on the art of generous hosting, and meat, fish, or eggs at the table are a must. As a host, it enables you to show off your creativity; as a guest, it tells you no trouble has been spared. In this edition, dishes such as Baked Eggs with Leeks (see page 108) would serve well for a weekend brunch or a light dinner, but at its most lavish, "secondi" include sumptuous combinations, such as Shrimp with Almonds and Bread Crumbs (see page 124), or rich Veneto-Style Liver (see page 146) that you would pair with a fine Barolo. These are dishes that speak of abundance and love.

Ham and Sage Frittata

Serves 2
Preparation 10 min
Cooking 15 min

— 6 eggs
— ¾ cup (4 oz/120 g) chopped cooked
   ham
— 6 fresh sage leaves or other herbs,
   such as parsley or chives, chopped
— 1 tablespoon freshly grated Parmesan
   cheese
— 2 tablespoons heavy (double) cream
— 2 tablespoons (1 oz/25 g) butter
— salt and pepper

Preheat the oven to 350°F/180°C/Gas Mark 4. Beat the eggs in a medium bowl, stir in the ham, sage, Parmesan, and cream, and season with salt and pepper.

Melt the butter in an 8-inch/20-cm ovenproof skillet or frying pan over medium heat. Once the butter is frothy, pour in the mixture and cook for 4–5 minutes until the bottom of the frittata is set. Put the skillet into the oven and cook for another 10 minutes, until the frittata is cooked through and golden on top. Turn out onto a plate and serve hot or cold.

Zucchini Frittata

Serves 2
Preparation 10 min
Cooking 20 min

— 2 tablespoons olive oil
— 2 tablespoons (1 oz/25 g) butter
— 3 cups (11 oz/300 g) thinly sliced
   zucchini (courgette)
— 6 eggs
— salt and pepper

Heat the oil and half the butter in an 8-inch/20-cm nonstick skillet or frying pan, add the zucchini (courgette), season with salt and pepper, and cook, stirring occasionally, for 10 minutes.

Meanwhile, lightly beat the eggs with a pinch of salt. Pour into the skillet. Cook for 5 minutes on each side, or until cooked through and lightly browned. Serve hot or cold.

Frittata with Aromatic Herbs

Serves 2
Preparation 5 min
Cooking 10 min

— 6 eggs
— 1 tablespoon finely chopped parsley
— 1 tablespoon finely chopped chives
— 1 tablespoon finely chopped tarragon
— 1 tablespoon finely chopped chervil
— 2 tablespoons (1 oz/25 g) butter
— salt and pepper

Lightly beat the eggs in a bowl, season with salt and pepper, and stir in the herbs.

Melt the butter in a nonstick skillet or frying pan over medium-high heat. Pour in the egg mixture and tilt and rotate the skillet to spread the mixture evenly. Cook for 10 seconds, then lift the cooked bottom with a spatula to let the uncooked egg run underneath. Continue cooking in this way until the frittata is just set underneath but the top is still soft and creamy.

Loosen the edge with a spatula (fish slice), tilt the skillet so that the frittata folds over itself, and slide it onto a serving plate. Serve immediately.

Soft-Boiled Eggs with Asparagus

Serves 4
Preparation 10 min
Cooking 10 min

— 4 eggs
— 1¾ lb/800 g asparagus, spears trimmed
— salt
— butter, melted, to serve

Immerse the eggs into a small saucepan of boiling water. Lower the heat to a simmer and cook for 3–4 minutes.

Meanwhile, bring a large saucepan of salted water to a boil, add the asparagus, bring back to a boil, and cook for 3 minutes, or until tender.

Put the eggs in egg cups, and serve with the hot asparagus and individual bowls of melted butter. To eat, dip the asparagus tip into the butter and then into the soft-boiled egg.

Baked Eggs with Leeks

Serves 4
Preparation 15 min
Cooking 25–30 min

— 1 lb 5 oz/600 g leeks, trimmed
— 4 tablespoons (2 oz/50 g) butter,
  plus extra for greasing
— pinch of freshly grated nutmeg
— 4 eggs
— salt and pepper

Halve the leeks lengthwise, then slice thinly. Melt the butter in a small skillet or frying pan, add the leeks, and cook over medium heat, stirring for 5 minutes, until softened. Season with salt and pepper to taste and sprinkle with the nutmeg. Stir well and add 3 tablespoons warm water, then cover and cook over medium heat for another 5 minutes.

Meanwhile, preheat the oven to 350°F/180°C/ Gas Mark 4 and grease four ramekins with butter. Divide the leeks among the ramekins, break an egg into each dish, and put in a deep baking pan. Pour boiling water into the pan to come half way up the ramekins, then bake in the oven for 15 minutes. Season lightly with pepper and serve.

Fried Mozzarella Sandwiches

Serves 4
Preparation 25 min
Cooking 5 min

— 8 small country-style (farmhouse) bread slices
— 5 oz/150 g mozzarella cheese, drained and sliced
— 2 eggs
— ¾ cup (6 fl oz/175 ml) milk
— all-purpose (plain) flour, for dusting
— 4 tablespoons olive oil
— 2 tablespoons (1 oz/25 g) butter
— salt and pepper

Put the slices of mozzarella on half the bread and top with the remaining bread to make sandwiches. Beat the eggs in a shallow dish with the milk and season with salt and pepper. Dust the sandwiches with flour and place in the beaten eggs, pressing down gently with a spatula (fish slice) until they have absorbed some of the mixture.

Heat the olive oil and butter in a large skillet or frying pan over medium-high heat, add the sandwiches, and cook for about 2 minutes on each side, until crisp and golden brown. Remove with a spatula and drain on paper towels. Serve hot.

Broiled Salmon with Rosemary

Serves 6
Preparation 15 min
Cooking 10 min

— 1¾ cups (3¼ oz/90 g) fresh rosemary
  leaves
— 6 (7-oz/200-g) salmon steaks or other
  fish, such as tuna steaks, or sea bass
— 3 tablespoons whipping cream or
  crème fraîche
— 1 quantity Mayonnaise
  (see page 226) or store-bought
— 2 tablespoons dry vermouth
— 1 cup (2 oz/50 g) chopped mixed
  herbs, such as flat-leaf parsley,
  dill, and thyme
— 1 dill pickle (pickled gherkin),
  finely chopped
— salt and pepper

Preheat the broiler (grill), line a broiler pan with aluminum foil, and sprinkle the rosemary leaves over it. Put the salmon steaks on top, season with salt and pepper, and broil (grill) for about 5 minutes on each side, or until cooked through and the flesh flakes easily with a fork.

Meanwhile, whip the cream, then fold it gently into the mayonnaise. Gently stir in the vermouth, herbs, and pickle (gherkin). To serve, put the salmon steaks on one side of a serving plate, slightly overlapping each other, and spoon the creamy mayonnaise sauce on the other side.

Tuna with Almonds, Pine Nuts, and Olives

Serves 4
Preparation 15 min
Cooking 20 min

— 2 tablespoons olive oil
— 4 (7-oz/200-g) tuna steaks
— scant ½ cup (3½ fl oz/100 ml) dry white wine
— 1 cup (3½ oz/100 g) pitted black olives, chopped
— ¼ cup (1½ oz/40 g) blanched almonds, chopped
— ¼ cup (1½ oz/40 g) pine nuts, chopped
— grated zest of 1 lemon
— ½ clove garlic, chopped
— 1 tablespoon chopped marjoram
— 1 tablespoon chopped thyme
— 1 tablespoon chopped flat-leaf parsley
— salt and pepper

Heat the oil in a skillet or frying pan, add the tuna, and cook over medium heat for 4 minutes on each side. Transfer the fish to a serving plate and keep warm.

Add the wine to the skillet, season with salt and pepper, and cook for about 8 minutes, or until most of the alcohol has evaporated.

Mix together the olives, almonds, pine nuts, lemon zest, garlic, marjoram, thyme, and parsley in a bowl, add to the skillet, and cook over low heat, stirring constantly, for 3 minutes. Remove from the heat, sprinkle the mixture over the tuna, and serve.

Hake in Green Sauce

Serves 4
Preparation 10 min
Cooking 15–20 min

— 4 (7-oz/200-g) hake steaks or fillets,
  or other fish, such as halibut or
  salmon steaks
— 2 tablespoons olive oil, plus extra
  for brushing
— 1 onion, finely chopped
— 1 celery stalk, plus a few leaves,
  finely chopped
— 2 flat-leaf parsley sprigs, chopped
— juice of 1 lemon, strained
— salt and pepper

Preheat the oven to 400°F/200°C/Gas Mark 6.
Brush the fish and an ovenproof dish with oil,
put the fish in it, season well, and bake for
15–20 minutes, or until cooked through and
the flesh flakes easily with a fork.

Meanwhile, heat the olive oil in a small
saucepan, add the onion and celery stalk, and
cook over medium heat, stirring occasionally,
for 5–10 minutes, or until softened. Season with
salt and pepper, remove from the heat, and keep
warm. Stir in the parsley, celery leaves, and lemon
juice. Serve the hake with this green sauce.

Branzino al Cartoccio

Sea Bass Baked in a Package

Serves 4
Preparation 15 min
Cooking 20–25 min

— olive oil, for brushing and serving
— 1 rosemary sprig
— 2 cloves garlic
— 1 (2¼-lb/1-kg) sea bass, spines
    trimmed, scaled, and cleaned
— 1 flat-leaf parsley sprig, chopped
— 1 lemon, sliced, plus extra for serving
— 1 onion, sliced into rings
— 2 scallions (spring onions), sliced
— 5 tablespoons dry white wine
— salt and pepper

Preheat the oven to 400°F/200°C/Gas Mark 6.
Cut out a sheet of parchment (baking) paper and
brush with olive oil.

Put the rosemary sprig and one of the garlic
cloves in the cavity of the sea bass, season
with salt and pepper, and place the fish on the
parchment paper. Slice the remaining garlic.

Sprinkle the fish with the parsley and cover with
the lemon slices, onion rings, scallions (spring
onions), and garlic slices. Spoon the wine over
the fish, fold over the parchment paper to enclose
it completely, and seal the edges.

Place on a baking sheet (baking tray) and bake for
20–25 minutes. Serve with olive oil, lemon slices,
and salt.

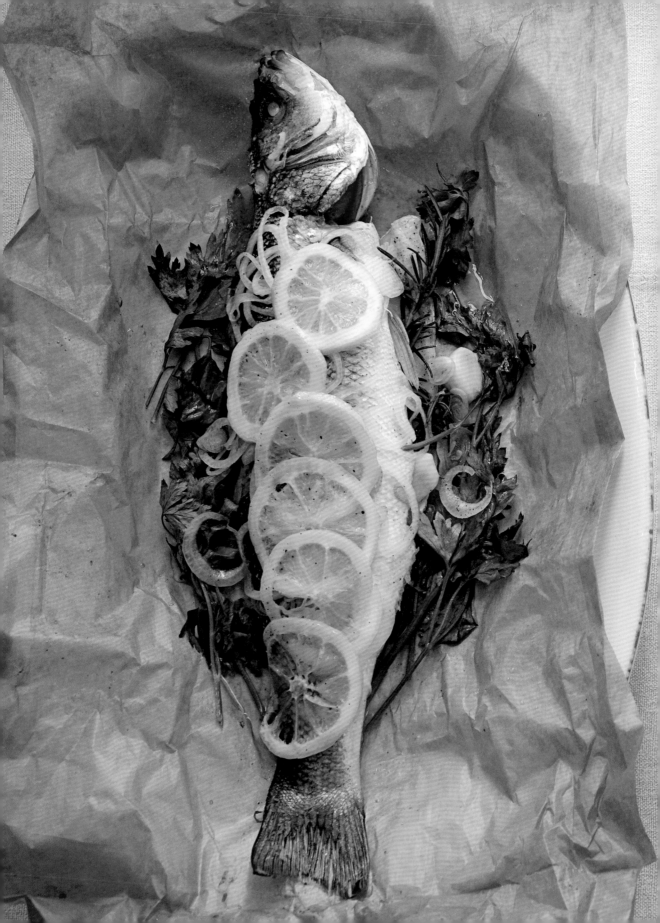

Sole with Thyme

Serves 4
Preparation 10 min
Cooking 15 min

— 4 sole, cleaned, trimmed, and skinned
— 3 tablespoons fresh thyme leaves
— ½ cup (4 fl oz/120 ml) olive oil, plus
  extra for drizzling
— juice of ½ lemon, strained
— salt and white pepper

Put the fish in a large saucepan, add water to cover and a pinch of salt, and bring just to a boil, then lower the heat and poach for about 5 minutes, or until tender and the flesh flakes easily with a fork. Drain and place on a serving dish.

Put the thyme leaves, a pinch of salt, and a pinch of white pepper into a bowl and gradually stir in the olive oil.

Drizzle the fish with olive oil and sprinkle with the lemon juice. Spoon the thyme sauce over the fish and keep in a cool place until ready to serve.

Delicious Sole

Serves 4
Preparation 15 min
Cooking 10 min

— 8 (3½-oz/100-g) sole fillets, skinned,
  or other fish, such as flounder, plaice,
  or turbot fillets
— all-purpose (plain) flour, for dusting
— 2 tablespoons (1 oz/25 g) butter
— 4 tablespoons olive oil
— generous 1 teaspoon Dijon mustard
— grated zest and juice of 1 small lemon
— 2 teaspoons coriander seeds, coarsely
  crushed
— 1 tablespoon chopped cilantro
  (coriander)
— ⅓ cup (1½ oz/40 g) blanched almonds,
  toasted and coarsely chopped
— salt and pepper

Lightly dust the fish fillets with flour, shaking off
the excess. Melt the butter with 2 tablespoons
of the oil in a skillet or frying pan over a medium
heat, add the sole fillets, in batches, and cook
for 2 minutes on each side. Season with salt and
pepper, then remove from the heat, transfer to
a serving plate and keep warm.

Whisk together the remaining oil, the mustard,
lemon zest and juice, coriander seeds, chopped
cilantro (coriander), and almonds in a bowl until
thoroughly combined, then pour into the skillet
and heat for a few minutes. Pour the sauce over
the fish and serve immediately.

Shrimp with Almonds and Bread Crumbs

Serves 4
Preparation 20 min
Cooking 10 min

— 5 tablespoons olive oil
— 1 small onion, chopped
— 1 clove garlic, chopped
— 1 bunch of flat-leaf parsley, chopped
— ½ teaspoon chili powder
— 1 lb 2 oz/500 g uncooked, peeled, and deveined shrimp (prawns)
— scant ½ cup (3½ fl oz /100 ml) dry white wine
— chili flakes (optional), to serve
— salt

For the almonds and bread crumbs
— 2 tablespoons olive oil
— scant 1 cup (3½ oz/100 g) chopped almonds
— 2 cups (3½ oz/100 g) fresh bread crumbs
— 1 heaped tablespoon grated Parmesan cheese
— pinch of chopped flat-leaf parsley
— salt

Heat the olive oil in a heavy pan, add the onion, garlic, and parsley, and cook over medium-high heat, stirring frequently, for a few minutes, then add the chili powder and shrimp (prawns). Cook, stirring continuously, for a few minutes, until the shrimp start to turn pink. Drizzle in the wine and cook for 4–5 minutes until evaporated. Remove from the heat and season to taste with salt.

Meanwhile, to make the almonds and bread crumbs, heat the olive oil in a skillet or frying pan. Add all the ingredients, season with salt, and cook over medium heat for 2–3 minutes, stirring constantly with a wooden spoon to prevent the mixture from burning. It will be ready when it is golden brown. Serve immediately with the shrimp, and chili flakes, if using.

Mussels Marinara

Serves 4
Preparation 10 min
Cooking 5 min

— 3¼ lb/1.5 kg mussels, scrubbed and
    beards removed
— 3 tablespoons finely chopped flat-leaf
    parsley
— pepper

Put the mussels into a large saucepan over high
heat with plenty of pepper but no water and cook
for about 5 minutes, until they open. Discard any
that remain closed. Drain, reserving the cooking
juices, and put the mussels in a deep serving dish.

Strain the cooking juices thorough a cheesecloth-
lined strainer (muslin-lined sieve) into a bowl. Stir
in the parsley, pour the mixture over the mussels,
and serve.

Skewered Sea Scallops

Serves 4
Preparation 15 min, plus marinating
Cooking 6 min

— juice of 2 limes, strained
— 1 clove garlic, crushed
— 16 sea scallops, shucked and cleaned,
  or other seafood, such as baby squid
— 1 green bell pepper
— 1 red bell pepper
— olive oil
— salt and pepper

Pour the lime juice into a shallow dish, season with salt and pepper, add the garlic and sea scallops, and let marinate in a cool place for 10 minutes. Preheat the broiler (grill).

Meanwhile, halve the bell peppers, remove the seeds and membranes, and chop into 8 pieces each.

Drain the sea scallops and thread 4 onto each of 4 skewers, alternate with the chunks of red and green bell peppers.

Brush with oil and broil (grill) for 2½–3 minutes on each side, or until opaque and cooked through. Remove from the heat, season with salt and pepper, transfer to a serving dish, and serve.

Chicken Roulades with Sage

Serves 4
Preparation 20 min
Cooking 25 min

— 4 skinless, boneless chicken breasts
— 8 fresh sage leaves
— 12 slices of pancetta or thick-cut bacon
— 2 tablespoons olive oil
— salt and pepper
— radicchio salad (optional), to serve

Lightly pound the chicken with a meat mallet or rolling pin. Put 2 sage leaves on each piece and season with salt and pepper. Roll up, wrap each roulade in 3 pancetta slices, and secure with toothpicks (cocktail sticks).

Heat the oil in a large skillet or frying pan, add the roulades, and cook over high heat for 5 minutes, turning frequently, until browned all over.

Cover and cook over low heat for about 20 minutes, or until cooked through. Serve with a radicchio salad.

Chicken, Anchovy, and Caper Roulades

Serves 4
Preparation 15 min
Cooking 30 min

— 4 skinless, boneless chicken breasts
— 8 canned anchovy fillets in oil, drained
— 3 tablespoons (1 oz/25 g) capers, drained and rinsed
— 2 tablespoons (1 oz/25 g) butter
— 1 tablespoon olive oil
— 1 onion, thinly sliced
— 4 tablespoons dry white wine
— salt and pepper

Lightly pound the chicken with a meat mallet or rolling pin. Divide the anchovies and capers among the chicken breasts, roll them up, and secure with toothpicks (cocktail sticks).

Heat the butter and oil in a medium skillet or frying pan, add the onion, and cook over low heat, stirring occasionally, for 3 minutes.

Add the roulades and cook over high heat for 5 minutes, turning frequently, until they are browned all over. Season to taste, pour in the wine, and cook for 2 minutes, until it has reduced slightly. Lower the heat, cover, and simmer for 20 minutes, or until cooked through. Transfer to a warm serving dish.

Beef Tenderloin with Fava Beans

Serves 4
Preparation 10 min
Cooking 10–20 min

— scant 1 cup (3½ oz/100 g) shelled frozen fava (broad) beans
— 4 (5-oz/140-g) beef tenderloin (fillet) steaks
— all-purpose (plain) flour, for dusting
— 3 tablespoons olive oil
— scant ½ cup (3½ fl oz/100 ml) dry white wine
— 1½ oz/45 g speck or prosciutto, cut into strips
— salt and pepper

Cook the fava (broad) beans in a saucepan of salted, boiling water for 3–5 minutes, until tender, then drain. Squeeze the beans out of their skins with a thumb and index finger and set aside.

Dust the steaks with seasoned flour, shaking off the excess. Heat the oil in a skillet or frying pan, add the steaks, and cook over medium-high heat, turning once, to your preference: 3 minutes for rare; 4 minutes for medium-rare; 6 minutes for medium; or 10 minutes for well done. Remove from the skillet, transfer to a serving dish, keep warm, and let rest.

Add the wine to the skillet and cook over high heat for a few minutes until reduced by half. Add the fava beans and speck, mix carefully, and cook for 1 minute to heat through. Season with salt and pepper, pour over the steaks, and serve immediately.

Steak with Mushrooms

Serves 4
Preparation 10 min
Cooking 15–30 min

— 4 tablespoons (2 oz/50 g) butter
— 1 shallot, finely chopped
— 3½ cups (9 oz/250 g) sliced
   mushrooms
— 5 tablespoons dry white wine
— 1 tablespoon tomato paste (purée)
— 2 tablespoons olive oil
— 4 (5-oz/140-g) beef tenderloin (fillet)
   steaks
— 1 sprig flat-leaf parsley, chopped
— salt
— 4 thick bread slices, crusts removed,
   (optional), to serve

Melt half the butter in a large saucepan,
add the shallot, and cook over low heat,
stirring occasionally, for 5 minutes. Add the
mushrooms, mix well, then add the wine,
increase the heat, and cook for 3–5 minutes,
or until it has evaporated.

Mix the tomato paste (purée) with 3 tablespoons
warm water, add the mixture to the pan, and
season lightly with salt. Cook, uncovered, for
5–10 minutes, or until the sauce is reduced
by half.

Melt the remaining butter with the oil in a
large skillet or frying pan, add the steaks, and
cook over medium–high heat, turning once, to
your preference: 3 minutes for rare; 4 minutes
for medium-rare; 6 minutes for medium; or
10 minutes for well done. Remove from the heat
and let rest for 3–5 minutes.

Season the steaks lightly with salt, spoon the
mushroom sauce over them, and sprinkle with
the parsley. Serve immediately, on toast, if using.

Steak Tartare

Serves 4
Preparation 25 min

— 1 lb/450 g lean steak, finely chopped
  or ground (minced)
— 4 egg yolks
— 1 onion, thinly sliced
— 1 tablespoon capers, drained and
  rinsed
— 2 tablespoons finely chopped flat-leaf
  parsley
— 4 canned anchovy fillets in oil, drained
  and chopped
— mild or medium French mustard
  (optional)
— olive oil and lemon wedges, to serve

Divide the steak among four dishes, shaping each portion into a mound. Make a shallow well in the center of each mound and gently place in a raw egg yolk.

Surround each mound with onion, capers, parsley, and anchovies. Serve with olive oil and lemon wedges. Each guest should season the meat to taste and can mix in the surrounding ingredients, using a fork. If you like, a little mustard may be used to spice up the dish.

Roman Saltimbocca

Serves 4
Preparation 5 min
Cooking 15 min

— 3½ oz/100 g prosciutto slices, halved
— 1 lb 2 oz/500 g veal scallops
   (escalopes)
— 8–10 fresh sage leaves
— 4 tablespoons (2 oz/50 g) butter
— scant ½ cup (3½ fl oz/100 ml)
   dry white wine
— salt

Put a slice of prosciutto on each scallop (escalope), put a sage leaf on top, and fasten with a toothpick (cocktail stick).

Melt the butter in a large skillet or frying pan and cook the veal over high heat on both sides until golden brown. Season with salt, pour in the wine, and cook until it has evaporated, then remove the toothpicks and serve.

Milanese Veal Chops

Serves 4
Preparation 15 min
Cooking 10 min

— 4 veal chops on the bone, 1 inch/
  2½ cm thick
— 1 egg
— 1½ cups (3 oz/80 g) fine bread crumbs
— 2 tablespoons (1 oz/30 g) butter
— 2 tablespoons olive oil
— salt

Pound the meat to an even thickness with a meat mallet or rolling pin. Beat the egg with a pinch of salt in a shallow dish. Spread out the bread crumbs in another shallow dish.

Melt the butter with the oil in a large skillet or frying pan. Dip each chop first in the beaten egg and then in the bread crumbs, pressing them on with your fingers.

Cook the chops over medium heat for about 5 minutes on each side, until golden brown. Remove with a spatula (fish slice) and drain on paper towels, then transfer to a warm serving dish. The chops go well with any vegetables served with butter, or with a fresh salad.

Scaloppine di Vitello al Marsala

Veal Scallops with Marsala

Serves 4
Preparation 5 min
Cooking 10–15 min

— 1 lb 2 oz/500 g veal scallops
  (escalopes)
— all-purpose (plain) flour, for dusting
— 6 tablespoons (3 oz/80 g) butter
— scant 2 cups (15 fl oz/450 ml) dry
  Marsala or Sherry
— 2 tablespoons chopped flat-leaf
  parsley, to serve
— salt and pepper

Dust the veal with seasoned flour, shaking off the excess. Melt the butter in a large saucepan and heat until it turns light brown in colour. Add the veal, in batches if necessary, and cook over high heat for 2–3 minutes on each side. Remove the veal from the pan, set aside on a plate, and keep warm.

Lower the heat and scrape up the sediment from the bottom of the pan with a wooden spoon, then pour in the Marsala, stir well, increase the heat, and simmer until reduced by about half. Spoon the sauce over the veal, garnish with the parsley, and serve.

Veneto-Style Liver

Serves 4
Preparation 15 min
Cooking 15 min

— 4–5 tablespoons olive oil
— 2 onions, thinly sliced
— ¾ cup (6 fl oz/175 ml) dry white wine
— 1 tablespoon chopped fresh flat-leaf
  parsley
— 1 lb 2 oz/500 g liver, such as calf's
  or pig's, sliced
— salt and pepper

Heat the oil in a large skillet or frying pan, add the onions, and cook over low heat, stirring occasionally, for about 10 minutes, until softened and lightly browned.

Add the wine, increase the heat to high, and cook until it has evaporated. Stir in the parsley and add the liver. Cook for 1–2 minutes on each side. Season to taste and transfer to a warm serving dish. Serve immediately.

Ten-Herb Sausages

Serves 4
Preparation 15 min
Cooking 20 min

— 1 tablsepoon olive oil
— 8 Italian sausages
— 1½ teaspoons rosemary, chopped
— 1½ teaspoons fresh sage leaves,
   chopped
— 1½ teaspoons basil leaves, chopped
— 1½ teaspoons thyme leaves, chopped
— 1½ teaspoons flat-leaf parsley,
   chopped
— 1½ teaspoons marjoram leaves,
   chopped
— 1½ teaspoons mint leaves, chopped
— 1½ teaspoons tarragon leaves, chopped
— 1 celery stalk (stick), finely diced
— 2 shallots, finely diced
— scant ½ cup (3½ fl oz /100 ml) dry
   white wine

The quantities of the various herbs, celery, and shallot used depend on individual taste, but it is best to go easy with the stronger herbs, such as rosemary.

Heat the oil and 2 tablespoons water in a large skillet or frying pan over medium heat. Prick the sausages, put them into the skillet, and cook, turning occasionally, for 10–15 minutes, until golden brown.

Add the herbs, celery, and shallots and cook for another few minutes. Pour in the wine and cook until it has evaporated, then serve.

Pork Chops in Butter and Sage

Serves 4
Preparation 5 min
Cooking 15 min

— 4 boneless pork loin chops, 1 inch/
  2½ cm thick
— 3 tablespoons (1½ oz/40 g) butter
— 6 fresh sage leaves
— salt and pepper

Flatten the chops slightly with a meat mallet or rolling pin.

Melt the butter in a skillet or frying pan, add the sage, and cook for 5 minutes, until light golden brown.

Add the chops and cook for 3–5 minutes on each side, until tender and cooked through. Season lightly with salt and pepper and serve immediately.

Belgian Endive with Prague Ham

Serves 4
Preparation 10 min
Cooking 15–20 min

— butter, for greasing
— 4 heads Belgian endive (chicory), trimmed
— 4 large Prague ham or other smoked ham slices
— 1 quantity Béchamel Sauce (see page 226) or store-bought
— pinch of freshly grated nutmeg
— ⅔ cup (¼ pint/150 ml) meat broth (stock)
— ¼ cup (1 oz/25 g) freshly grated Parmesan cheese
— salt and pepper

Preheat the oven to 400°F/200°C/Gas Mark 6. Grease an ovenproof dish with butter.

Wrap each head of Belgian endive (chicory) in a slice of ham and put in the prepared dish. Season with salt and pepper, spoon in the béchamel sauce, and sprinkle with the nutmeg. Add the broth (stock) and sprinkle with the Parmesan.

Bake for 15–20 minutes. Remove the dish from the oven, let rest for 5 minutes, and serve.

Sides

No table setting would be complete without some colorfully robust plates of food designed to complement and enhance the "secondi." Led by the seasons, "contorni" offer cooks a chance to show off the rich bounty of the land. Without exception, these dishes are special enough to steal the limelight, and they would make for a sensational vegetarian menu in their own right. Spicy Broccoli with Yogurt (see page 166), Treviso Radicchio Salad with Orange (see page 182), and Fennel, Celery, and Apple Salad (see page 188), will transport anyone eating it straight into the heart of the Italian countryside.

Parmesan Asparagus

Serves 4
Preparation 10 min
Cooking 5 min

— 2¼ lb/1 kg asparagus, spears trimmed
— 1 cup (3 oz/ 80 g) freshly grated
   Parmesan cheese
— 4 tablespoons (2 oz/50 g) butter
— salt

Cook the asparagus in a saucepan of salted, boiling water for 4–5 minutes, or until tender. Drain and pat dry gently. Arrange in a warm serving dish. Sprinkle with the Parmesan.

Melt the butter, season with a little salt, and pour onto the asparagus. Serve immediately.

White Bean and Asparagus Salad

Serves 4–6
Preparation 15 min
Cooking 5 min

— 1 bunch (12 oz/340 g) thin young asparagus
— 1 cup (9 oz/250 g) drained and rinsed, canned cannellini beans
— 5 tablespoons extra virgin olive oil
— juice of ½ lemon, strained
— 1 small bunch parsley, finely chopped
— salt and freshly ground white pepper

Trim the asparagus spears to the same length and tie in a bundle with kitchen twine (string). Bring a tall saucepan of lightly salted water to a boil. Add the asparagus, standing the bundle upright with the tips protruding above the water level. Cover and simmer for 3 minutes, or until tender.

Lift out the asparagus, rinse under cold water to stop the cooking process, and drain on paper towels. Cut the asparagus in half.

Put the beans into a serving dish. Whisk together the oil, lemon juice, and parsley in a bowl and season with salt and white pepper. Drizzle the dressing over the beans, put the asparagus pieces on top, toss gently, and serve.

Summer Cannellini Beans

Serves 4–6
Preparation 10 min
Cooking 20 min

— 2 fresh tomatoes
— 3 tablespoons olive oil
— 1 clove garlic
— 1 eggplant (aubergine), cut into
  ½ inch/1 cm dice
— 1 yellow bell pepper, halved, seeded,
  and cut into ½ inch/1 cm dice
— 1½ cups (12 oz/350 g) drained and
  rinsed, canned cannellini beans
— zest of ½ lemon
— 4 basil leaves, chopped
— 1 sprig flat-leaf parsley, chopped
— salt and pepper

Blanch the tomatoes in a heatproof bowl of boiling water for a few seconds, then peel, seed, and chop.

Heat the oil in a large saucepan, add the garlic, and cook for 2 minutes, or until browned, then remove and discard.

Add the eggplant (aubergine) and bell pepper to the pan and cook over high heat for 2–3 minutes. Add the tomatoes and beans, cover, lower the heat, and cook for 5 minutes. Season with salt and pepper and cook, uncovered, for another 5 minutes.

Remove the pan from the heat, transfer the mixture to a warm serving dish, and sprinkle with the lemon zest, basil, and parsley. Mix well and serve.

Peas with Pancetta

Serves 4
Preparation 5 min
Cooking 15 min

— 3½ cups (1lb 2 oz/500 g) shelled peas, fresh or frozen
— 3 tablespoons (1½ oz/40 g) butter
— 3½ oz/100 g smoked pancetta or thick-cut bacon, cut into strips
— salt

Cook the peas in a saucepan of salted, boiling water for 3–5 minutes, or until tender, then drain well and set aside.

Melt the butter in the pan over medium heat, add the pancetta, and cook for 10 minutes, or until golden brown and tender. Add the peas and stir until combined. Transfer to a warm serving dish.

Brussels Sprouts with Almonds

Serves 4
Preparation 10 min
Cooking 10–15 min

— 1 lb 5 oz/600 g Brussels sprouts, trimmed
— 4 tablespoons (2 oz/50 g) butter
— ¼ cup (1½ oz/40 g) blanched almonds
— 1 clove garlic
— thinly pared zest of 1 lemon, chopped
— ½ cup (1 oz/25 g) bread crumbs
— salt and pepper

Cook the Brussels sprouts in a saucepan of salted, boiling water for 5–10 minutes, or until just tender, then drain thoroughly. Transfer to a serving dish and keep warm.

Melt half of the butter in a skillet or frying pan over medium heat, add the almonds and garlic, and cook for a few minutes. Add the lemon zest, season with salt and pepper, and remove from the heat. Remove and discard the garlic. Pour over the Brussels sprouts.

Melt the remaining butter in the skillet, add the bread crumbs and cook, stirring continuously, until golden. Spoon over the Brussels sprouts and serve.

Spicy Broccoli with Yogurt

Serves 4
Preparation 10 min
Cooking 5 min

— 2¼ lb/1 kg purple or green baby
   (sprouting) broccoli, divided into
   florets
— 1 sprig parsley, chopped
— 1 clove garlic, chopped
— 1 mild red chile, seeded and chopped
— scant ½ cup (3½ fl oz/100 ml) low-fat
   plain (natural) yogurt
— pinch of dry mustard (mustard powder)
— salt

Parboil the broccoli in a saucepan of salted,
boiling water for a few minutes until just tender,
then drain well and transfer to a large salad bowl.

Combine the parsley, garlic, chile, and yogurt in
a bowl, stir in the mustard, and season with salt
to taste. Pour the sauce over the broccoli and
serve warm.

Artichokes with Parmesan

Serves 4
Preparation 20 min, plus soaking
Cooking 25 min

— juice of 1 lemon, strained
— 8 globe artichokes
— 4 tablespoons olive oil
— ⅔ cup (2 oz/50 g) grated Parmesan
  cheese
— 1 tablespoon chopped parsley
— salt and pepper

Fill a bowl halfway with water and stir in the lemon juice. Trim the artichoke stems and remove any coarse outer leaves and the chokes, then add the artichokes immediately to the acidulated water to prevent discoloration. Let soak for 15 minutes, then drain and cut into thin wedges.

Heat 2 tablespoons of the oil in a skillet or frying pan, add the artichokes, and cook over low heat, stirring and turning occasionally, for 15 minutes. Meanwhile, preheat the oven to 375°F/190°C/ Gas Mark 5.

Remove the pan from the heat. Transfer the artichokes to a baking pan, sprinkle with the remaining oil, cheese, and parsley, and season lightly with salt and pepper. Bake for 10 minutes and serve immediately.

Carote Novelle in Salsa d'Erbe

Baby Carrots in Herb Sauce

Serves 6
Preparation 10 min
Cooking 25–30 min

— 1¾ lb/800 g baby carrots, trimmed
— 3 tablespoons (1½ oz/40 g) butter
— 1 tablespoon olive oil
— 1 clove garlic, peeled
— 2 tablespoons chopped mixed herbs,
   such as parsley, basil, and marjoram
— 4 tablespoons heavy (double) cream
— salt and pepper

Bring a saucepan of lightly salted water to a boil. Add the carrots and cook for 10 minutes, or until tender, then drain.

Meanwhile, melt the butter with the oil in a skillet or frying pan over low heat. Add the garlic and cook, stirring frequently, over medium heat for 5 minutes, or until golden brown. Remove the garlic and discard.

Add the carrots to the skillet and cook for 2 minutes, then add the chopped herbs, season with salt and pepper, and stir in the cream.

Simmer gently for 10–15 minutes, until the sauce has reduced. If the sauce seems a little too thick, stir in a little lukewarm water or milk. Remove from the heat and serve warm.

Braised Scallions

Serves 4
Preparation 10 min
Cooking 30 min

— 2 tablespoons (1 oz/25 g) butter
— 2 tablespoons finely chopped
   mixed herbs, such as thyme,
   marjoram, and sage
— 2 oz/50 g pancetta or thick-cut bacon,
   cut into thin strips
— 1 lb 2 oz/500 g large scallions
   (spring onions), thickly sliced
— salt and pepper

Melt the butter with the herbs in a skillet or
frying pan. Add the pancetta, and white and
light green parts of the scallions (spring onions),
and cook over low heat, stirring continuously,
for 10 minutes.

Add the dark green parts of the scallions
and cook, stirring occasionally, for another
10 minutes.

Add 2 tablespoons of hot water and simmer for
10 minutes, until the scallions are tender and all
the liquid has evaporated. Season with salt and
pepper and serve immediately.

New Potatoes with Rosemary

Serves 4
Preparation 5 min
Cooking 25 min

— 1½ lb/675 g new potatoes
— 2 tablespoons (1 oz/25 g) butter
— scant ½ cup (3½ fl oz /100 ml)
  olive oil
— 1 sprig rosemary
— 1 clove garlic
— salt

Bring a saucepan of lightly salted water to a boil, add the potatoes, and simmer for 10 minutes, then drain.

Meanwhile, heat the butter and oil in a large skillet or frying pan. Add the rosemary, garlic, and potatoes, stir, and cover. Cook over medium heat, stirring occasionally, for 15 minutes, or until golden brown.

Remove and discard the garlic and rosemary, sprinkle with salt, and serve.

Garbanzo Bean and Radicchio Salad

Serves 4
Preparation 15 min
Cooking 10 min

— 4–5 new potatoes
— 2 heads radicchio, preferably Treviso
— scant 1 cup (5 oz/150 g) drained
    and rinsed, canned garbanzo beans
    (chickpeas)
— 2½ oz/65 g Parmesan cheese
— 6 tablespoons olive oil
— 1 tablespoon balsamic vinegar
— salt and pepper

Bring a small saucepan of lightly salted water to a boil, add the potatoes, and simmer for 10 minutes, then drain, cool, and slice into rounds.

Meanwhile, cut the radicchio into large pieces and put into a salad bowl. Add the garbanzo beans (chickpeas) and potatoes.

Shave off some of the Parmesan and set aside for the garnish.

Grate the remaining Parmesan into a bowl. Add the oil, vinegar, and a pinch of salt and whisk to a smooth dressing. Pour the dressing over the salad and stir well. Sprinkle with the Parmesan shavings, season with pepper, and serve.

Insalata con Melagrana

Mixed Salad with Pomegranate

Serves 4
Preparation 25 min

— 1 pomegranate
— 2 carrots, cut into thin sticks
— 1 bunch mâche (lamb's lettuce), trimmed
— 1 bunch arugula (rocket), trimmed
— 1 bunch young spinach, trimmed
— scant ½ cup (3½ fl oz/100 ml) olive oil
— 1–2 tablespoons balsamic vinegar
— juice of ½ orange, strained
— salt

Cut a thin slice from one end of the pomegranate, stand it upright, and cut down through the skin at intervals. Holding the pomegranate over a bowl, bend the sections back, and scrape the seeds into the bowl with your fingers. Remove all traces of pith and membranes.

Put the carrots, mâche (lamb's lettuce), arugula (rocket), and spinach into a salad bowl.

Whisk together the oil, vinegar, and orange juice in a small bowl and season with salt to taste. Pour the dressing over the salad and toss. Sprinkle with the pomegranate seeds and serve.

Red Cabbage, Pancetta, and Roquefort Salad

Serves 6
Preparation 15 min
Cooking 20 min

— 1 small red cabbage, cored and finely shredded
— ½ cup (4 fl oz/120 ml) red wine vinegar
— 4 tablespoons olive oil
— 9 oz/250 g smoked pancetta or thick-cut bacon, diced
— 6 slices soft white bread, crusts removed, cut into small squares
— arugula (rocket), to serve
— ¾ cup (6 fl oz/175 ml) olive oil
— 3 tablespoons white wine vinegar
— 1 tablespoon Dijon mustard
— 3½ oz/100 g Roquefort or other blue cheese, such as Gorgonzola or Stilton, diced
— salt and pepper

Put the cabbage into a heatproof bowl. Pour the vinegar into a small saucepan and bring to a boil. Remove from the heat and pour over the cabbage.

Heat 1 tablespoon of the oil in a large skillet or frying pan. Add the pancetta and cook over medium-high heat, stirring frequently, for 8–10 minutes until crisp. Remove with a slotted spoon and set aside.

Heat the remaining oil in the skillet. Add the bread squares, in batches if necessary, and cook over medium heat, stirring and turning occasionally, for 4–5 minutes, or until golden and crisp. Remove with a spatula (fish slice) and drain on paper towels.

To make the vinaigrette, whisk together the oil, vinegar, and mustard in a bowl, and season with salt and pepper.

Drain the cabbage and transfer to a serving dish. Drizzle with the vinaigrette, top with the pancetta, croutons, Roquefort, arugula (rocket), and toss. Serve immediately.

Treviso Radicchio Salad with Orange

Serves 4
Preparation 15 min

— juice of 2 oranges, strained
— 3–4 tablespoons olive oil
— 1 teaspoon lemon juice (optional)
— 4 heads Treviso radicchio,
 cut into thin wedges
— salt and pepper

Whisk together the orange juice and oil in a bowl and season with salt and pepper to taste. Add a few drops of lemon juice to sharpen the taste if the orange juice is too sweet.

Put the radicchio into a bowl and pour the orange dressing over it, then toss gently, and serve.

The unusual sweet-and-sour combination of this salad makes it a suitable side dish for boiled fish or mixed boiled meats.

Radish Salad with Olives

Serves 4
Preparation 10 min

— 6 red radishes, trimmed
— juice of 1 lemon, strained
— 2 cups (3½ oz/100 g) mâche
  (lamb's lettuce)
— 10 pitted black olives
— extra virgin olive oil, for drizzling
— salt

Cut the radishes into thin slices, put into a salad bowl, and sprinkle with the lemon juice. Add the mâche (lamb's lettuce) and olives, drizzle with oil, and season with salt to taste. Mix gently and serve.

Orange Salad

Serves 4–6
Preparation 30 min

— 4 oranges
— 2 fennel bulbs, thinly sliced,
  fronds reserved
— ½ cup (2¼ oz/60 g) pitted black olives

For the dressing
— 5 tablespoons olive oil
— juice of ½ lemon, strained
— 2 tablespoons chopped flat-leaf
  parsley
— reserved fennel fronds (see above)
— 1 teaspoon fennel seeds (optional)
— salt and pepper

First make the dressing. Whisk together the olive oil, lemon juice, parsley, fennel fronds, and fennel seeds, if using, in a bowl and season to taste with salt and pepper.

Cut off the peel from the oranges, removing all traces of bitter white pith. Cut the flesh into rounds, put them into a large salad bowl, and add the fennel and olives. Mix well. Drizzle the dressing over the salad to taste, and serve.

Fennel, Celery, and Apple Salad

Serves 4
Preparation 20 min

— 2 fennel bulbs, fronds reserved
— 2 green apples
— 2 celery hearts
— ⅔ cup (¼ pint/150 ml) plain
  (natural) yogurt
— 2 tablespoons snipped chives
— reserved fennel fronds,
  to garnish (optional)
— salt and pepper

Thinly slice the fennel and core and thinly slice the apples. Slice the celery hearts into rounds. Combine the fennel, apples, and celery hearts in a shallow salad bowl.

Combine the yogurt and chives in a bowl, season with salt and pepper, and add to the salad. Toss lightly, sprinkle over the fennel fronds, if using, and serve.

Insalata di Pollo con Sedano Rapa

Chicken and Celeriac Salad

Serves 6–8
Preparation 20 min

— 2 cups (11 oz/300 g) cooked chicken, shredded
— 1 (1 lb 7 oz/650 g) celeriac, peeled and cut into thin sticks
— 1 quantity Mayonnaise (see page 226) or store-bought
— 3 tablespoons plain (natural) yogurt
— 1–2 teaspoons Dijon mustard, according to taste
— 1 sprig flat-leaf parsley, chopped, to garnish (optional)
— salt and pepper

Put the chicken and celeriac into a salad bowl. Combine the mayonnaise, yogurt, and mustard in another bowl and season to taste. Gently stir the dressing into the salad, sprinkle with the parsley, if using, and serve.

Shrimp and Corn Salad

Serves 4
Preparation 10 min
Cooking 5–6 min

— 1½ cups (9 oz/250 g) canned corn kernels, drained
— 11 oz (300 g) uncooked, peeled and deveined jumbo shrimp (king prawns)
— extra virgin olive oil
— juice of 1 lemon, strained (optional)
— 1 sprig flat-leaf parsley, chopped, to garnish (optional)
— salt and pepper

Put the drained corn kernels into a salad bowl.

Cook the shrimp (prawns) in a saucepan of salted, boiling water for 5–6 minutes, until the shrimp turn pink, then drain and add to the corn. Toss together, then drizzle with oil and lemon juice, if using, and season to taste.

Let cool to room temperature and sprinkle with parsley, if using, before serving.

Desserts and Beverages

The very sweet pastries and jams of Italian dolci tend
to be saved as breakfast treats for the weekend, along
with fruit fritters and smoothies. Cinnamon Cookies
(see page 214) work wonderfully as an afternoon
pick-me-up with a devilishly strong espresso—the
combination of sweet and bitter is profoundly good.
By contrast, after-dinner desserts, such as Zabaglione
(see page 196) or Plums in Wine (see page 204), are
of the featherlight variety with just a hint of sweetness.

Zabaglione

Serves 4
Preparation 10 min
Cooking 5–10 min

— 4 egg yolks
— ¼ cup (2 oz/50 g) superfine (caster) sugar
— ½ cup (4 fl oz/120 ml) sweet Marsala, dry white wine, or Sherry

Beat the egg yolks with the sugar in a heatproof bowl with an electric mixer (whisk) until pale and fluffy, then pour and stir in the Marsala, a little at a time.

Place the bowl over a saucepan of barely simmering water and cook over low heat, whisking continuously, until the mixture starts to rise. Do not let the mixture boil. Once the mixture has doubled in size and a ribbon trail is left on the top when the mixer is lifted, remove from the heat and serve warm or cold in glasses.

Alternatively, zabaglione may be used as a sauce on coffee or hazelnut ice cream.

Forest Fruit Gratin with Zabaglione

Serves 4
Preparation 10 min
Cooking 10 min

— 1 lb 2 oz/500 g mixed berries, such as blackberries, raspberries, blueberries, and hulled strawberries
— 3 egg yolks
— ⅓ cup (2½ oz/65 g) superfine (caster) sugar
— 2 tablespoons Grand Marnier, or other orange liqueur
— finely grated zest of ½ lemon

Cut any large berries in half and divide them among 4 individual flameproof dishes, or alternatively spread them out on the bottom of a large flameproof baking dish.

Preheat the broiler (grill).

Beat the egg yolks with the sugar and Grand Marnier in a heatproof bowl. Place the bowl over a saucepan of barely simmering water and cook over low heat, whisking continuously, for 5–8 minutes, until thickened. Do not let the mixture boil.

Remove the bowl from the heat, stir in the grated lemon zest, and pour the zabaglione over the fruit. Put the dishes under the broiler and cook for 1–2 minutes, or until golden brown. Serve warm or cold.

Caramel

Makes 3 fl oz/90 ml
Preparation 5 min
Cooking 15 min

— ½ cup (3½ oz/100 g) superfine (caster)
  sugar

Rinse out a small, stainless steel saucepan with cold water, add the sugar, and pour in ½ cup (4 fl oz/120 ml) warm water.

Cook over medium-low heat, stir until the sugar has dissolved completely, then wait for it to turn golden brown while it simmers. This may take up to 15 minutes. Watch carefully to ensure it doesn't burn. The caramel is ready when it drips slowly off the back of a spoon and thickens as it cools. Take care when checking if the caramel is ready, as it will be extremely hot.

Pour immediately over ice cream or fresh fruit.

Blueberries in Syrup

Makes 2¹/₃ cups (1 lb 5 oz/ 600 g)
Preparation 5 min
Cooking 15 min, plus cooling

— 4½ cups (1 lb 2 oz/500 g) blueberries
— 2½ cups (1 lb 2 oz/500 g) superfine
  (caster) sugar
— 5 tablespoons grappa or vodka

Put the blueberries into a large saucepan, add 5 tablespoons water, and heat gently on the lowest heat for 10 minutes.

Add the sugar and cook, stirring gently, until it has dissolved completely. Remove from the heat and let cool slightly. Then sprinkle with the grappa and let cool completely.

Spoon the berries and syrup into one or two sterilized jars, seal the tops, and store in the refrigerator for up to 2 weeks.

Use for decorating a variety of desserts and for serving with ice cream.

Desserts and Beverages

Prugne al Vino

Plums in Wine

Serves 6
Preparation 10 min
Cooking 20 min, plus cooling

— 3 cups (1¼ pints/750 ml) sweet
  rosé wine
— 1 cinnamon stick
— ⅔ cup (4 oz/120 g) superfine (caster)
  sugar
— thinly pared zest of ½ lemon,
  finely chopped
— 12–18 plums, pitted

Pour the wine into a large saucepan, add the cinnamon, sugar, and lemon zest, and bring to a boil, stirring until the sugar has dissolved.

Add the plums and simmer for 10 minutes.

Transfer the plums and liquid into a heatproof glass dish and let cool slightly. Remove the cinnamon stick and serve.

Desserts and Beverages

Pere al Cioccolato

Pears in Chocolate

Serves 4
Preparation 15 min
Cooking 15 min

— 2 tablespoons (1 oz/25 g) superfine
   (caster) sugar
— 4 ripe pears
— 3½ oz/100 g semisweet (plain)
   chocolate, broken into pieces
— 1½ tablespoons (¾ oz/20 g) unsalted
   butter
— 1–2 tablespoons pear brandy (optional)

Preheat the oven to 325°F/160°C/Gas Mark 3.
Sprinkle half the sugar evenly over the bottom
of an ovenproof dish.

Peel, halve, and core the pears, put them into the
dish, and sprinkle with the remaining sugar. Bake
for 15 minutes.

Meanwhile, melt the chocolate and butter in
a heatproof bowl set over a saucepan of barely
simmering water. Add the pear brandy, if using,
and stir until smooth and velvety. Pour the
chocolate sauce over the pears and serve warm.

Apple Fritters

Serves 4
Preparation 15 min
Cooking 15–20 min

— 4 apples
— scant ½ cup (3½ fl oz/100 ml) rum
   or juice of 2 lemons, strained
— sunflower oil, for deep-frying
— 1 quantity Sweet Fritter Batter (see
   page 228)
— confectioners' (icing) sugar, for dusting

Peel and core the apples, then cut into fairly thick slices, about 4–5 per apple, and sprinkle with the rum or lemon juice.

Heat plenty of oil to 350°F/180°C in a large, deep skillet or frying pan, or until a drop of the batter turns golden brown in 20 seconds.

Dip the apple slices in the batter, making sure they are evenly covered. Carefully place the apple slices into the skillet, a few at a time, and fry for 1–2 minutes on each side, or until light golden brown.

Remove with a slotted spoon, drain on paper towels, and transfer to a warm serving dish. Dust with plenty of confectioners' (icing) sugar.

Pineapple, peach, pear, and other fruit fritters may be prepared in the same way.

Chocolate Crêpes

Serves 4–6
Preparation 5 min
Cooking 30 min

— vegetable oil, for frying
— 1 quantity Crêpes batter (see page 229)
— 2 tablespoons milk
— 9 oz/250 g semisweet (plain) chocolate, broken into pieces
— 2 tablespoons (1 oz/25 g) unsalted butter
— whipped heavy (double) cream, to serve

Heat 1 teaspoon of oil in a skillet or frying pan until hot. Add a ladleful of the crêpe batter and swirl the skillet so that the batter covers the base. Cook for 1 minute, or until golden underneath. Flip the crêpe and cook for another 30 seconds–1 minute until golden underneath. Transfer to a plate. Repeat with the remaining batter, and stack them, separated with wax (greaseproof) paper, on a plate. Keep warm.

Melt the milk, chocolate, and butter together in a heatproof bowl set over a saucepan of barely simmering water. Stir until smooth and velvety.

Spread the chocolate mixture over the crêpes while they are still warm.

Fold each crêpe into a half-moon shape, arrange, slightly overlapping, on a serving dish, and serve with the whipped cream.

Crêpes with Preserves

Serves 6
Preparation 10 min
Cooking 30 min

— 1 teaspoon vegetable oil
— 1 quantity Crêpes batter (see page 229)
— ½ cup (5 oz/150 g) apricot preserves or jam
— zest of 1 orange
— ¼ cup (2 oz/50 g) superfine (caster) sugar, plus extra for sprinkling
— 4 tablespoons (2 fl oz/50 ml) brandy

Heat 1 teaspoon of oil in a skillet or frying pan until hot. Add a ladleful of the crêpe batter and swirl the skillet so that the batter covers the base. Cook for 1 minute, or until golden underneath. Flip the crêpe and cook for another 30 seconds–1 minute until golden underneath. Transfer to a plate. Repeat with the remaining batter, and stack them, separated with wax (greaseproof) paper, on a plate. Keep warm.

Put the apricot preserves, orange zest, sugar, and ⅔ cup (5 fl oz/150 ml) water into a small saucepan and bring to a boil. Cook, stirring continuously, for a few minutes until thickened, then remove from the heat and add the brandy.

Spread a little of the apricot mixture on each crêpe and fold into four. Transfer to a serving dish, sprinkle with sugar, and serve warm.

Cinnamon Cookies

Makes 30
Preparation 20–25 min
Cooking 15 min, plus cooling

— 2 cups (9 oz/250 g) all-purpose (plain) flour, plus extra for dusting
— 1 teaspoon baking powder
— ¼ teaspoon salt
— ⅔ cup (4½ oz/130 g) superfine (caster) sugar, plus 2 tablespoons for rolling
— 1 teaspoon ground cinnamon, plus 1 tablespoon for rolling, and 1 teaspoon for dusting (optional)
— zest of 1 lemon, grated
— 5 tablespoons olive oil
— 3 eggs, beaten

Preheat the oven to 350°F/180°C/Gas Mark 4. Sift (sieve) the flour with the baking powder and salt into a large bowl. Stir in the sugar, cinnamon, and lemon zest. Make a well in the center, pour in the oil and eggs, and mix until well combined. You might need to squeeze the dough together with your hands.

Line a baking sheet with parchment (baking) paper. On a plate, mix together the ground cinnamon and the sugar for rolling. Shape the dough into balls, roll in the cinnamon-sugar mixture, then transfer to the baking sheet and flatten slightly.

Bake for about 15 minutes, or until golden brown on the edges. Remove the baking sheet from the oven, let the cookies cool slightly, then transfer to a wire rack to cool completely.

Tidy up the edges with a cookie cutter and dust with cinnamon, if preferred.

Chocolate and Pear Tart

Serves 8
Preparation 20 min
Cooking 15 min, plus cooling

— 1 large precooked, sweet pie crust
  (pastry case)
— 4 ripe pears
— 2 tablespoons superfine (caster) sugar
— 4 tablespoons Grand Marnier, or other
  orange liqueur
— 4½ oz/130 g semisweet (plain)
  chocolate, broken into pieces
— 4 tablespoons (2 oz/50 g) unsalted
  butter
— scant ½ cup (3½ fl oz/100 ml)
  heavy (double) cream
— ¼ cup (1 oz/25 g) blanched almonds,
  chopped

Preheat the oven to 325°F/160°C/Gas Mark 3.
Sprinkle half the sugar evenly over the bottom
of an ovenproof dish.

Peel, halve, and core the pears, put them into
the dish, and sprinkle with the Grand Marnier,
and remaining sugar. Bake for 15 minutes.

Meanwhile, put the chocolate, butter, and
1 tablespoon water into a small saucepan
and melt over low heat for 5–8 minutes. Stir,
remove the pan from the heat, and let cool
for 10 minutes.

Remove the pears from the oven and transfer
to the pie crust.

Whip the cream until stiff and fold into the
chocolate mixture. Spread the chocolate topping
over the pears, sprinkle with the almonds,
and serve.

Jam Tart

Serves 4
Preparation 15 min
Cooking 25–30 min

— 1 lb 2 oz/500 g ready-to-bake pie
   dough (shortcrust pastry)
— all-purpose (plain) flour, for dusting
— 1 cup (11 oz/ 350 g) black cherry jam,
   preserves, or spread
— 1 egg, beaten
— confectioners' (icing) sugar, to serve

Preheat the oven to 375°F/190°C/Gas Mark 5.
Roll out the dough (pastry) on a floured work
surface to about ¼ inch/½ cm thick. Use to
line a 6¼ x 9-inch/16 x 23-cm pie dish and
trim the edges.

Fill the shell (case) with jam, spreading it out
evenly.

Re-roll the remaining dough and cut into ½-inch-/
1-cm-thick strips. Use these to create a lattice
pattern on top of the jam, sticking them to the
pastry with a little of the beaten egg.

Then twist the remaining strips and use to make a
border, brushing the pastry underneath with more
of the egg to help the twists stick.

Brush the pastry all over with the egg and bake for
25–30 minutes, until the tart is golden. Dust with
confectioners' (icing) sugar to serve.

Summer Smoothie

Serves 4
Preparation 10 min

— 2½ cups (1 pint/600 ml) low-fat plain (natural) yogurt
— 2½ cups (1 pint/600 ml) crushed ice
— ¼ cup (2 oz/50 g) superfine (caster) sugar
— juice of ½ small lemon, strained
— 4 daisies, or other edible flowers, such as nasturtiums, pansies, or rose petals, to decorate (optional)

Pour the yogurt into a blender, add the crushed ice, sugar, and lemon juice, and process at medium speed until smooth and even.

Divide the smoothie among 4 glasses, decorate each with a daisy, and serve.

Strawberry Smoothie

Serves 4
Preparation 15 min, plus soaking

— 2 tablespoons white wine vinegar
— 14 oz/400 g strawberries
— superfine (caster) sugar, to taste
— 3 cups (1¼ pints/750 ml) milk

Chill 4 glasses in the refrigerator. Stir the vinegar into a medium bowl of water. Add the strawberries, without hulling them, and let soak for about 10 minutes. Drain the strawberries well and hull them. Put them into a blender and blend to a puree.

Taste and add a little sugar, if necessary. Add the milk gradually and blend briefly again to mix. Pour into the chilled glasses and serve.

Basics

These recipes are the secret weapon of any home cook, elevating even the most simple of dishes to something special. Once you've mastered how to make a perfect tomato sauce (see page 32) or deeply aromatic pesto (see page 48), both of which are wonderful for pasta or pizza, you'll never buy store-bought again. You'll be amazed, too, how adding a few unlikely combinations, such as Fettuccine with Walnut Sauce (see page 58) or Sage Butter (see page 228), to your repertoire will transform humble chicken or pork chops into something extraordinary. Whether you're whipping up homemade Mayonnaise (see page 226) to serve with shrimp, or Crêpes (see page 229) for breakfast, these superfast, pantry basics will ensure your midweek meals will never be dull again.

Mayonnaise

Makes 1 cup (8 fl oz/250 ml)
Preparation 20 min

— 1 egg, plus 1 egg yolk
— ½ teaspoon dry mustard
  (mustard powder)
— scant 1 cup (7 fl oz/200 ml)
  sunflower oil
— 2 tablespoons lemon juice
  or white wine vinegar
— salt and ground white pepper

Put the whole egg, egg yolk, and mustard into a food processor, season with salt and pepper, and add 2 tablespoons of the oil and a drop of the lemon juice or vinegar. Process for a few seconds at maximum speed.

Drizzle half the remaining oil through the feed tube with the motor running. Add 1 teaspoon of the lemon juice or vinegar, then drizzle in the remaining oil.

When the ingredients are thoroughly mixed, adjust the seasoning and lemon juice or vinegar to taste, and process to combine. For a lighter, whiter mayonnaise, whisk in 1 tablespoon boiled hot water.

Store in the refrigerator for up to one week. Serve with boiled or roasted meat, raw or cooked vegetables, or as a garnish.

Béchamel Sauce

Makes scant 2 cups (15 fl oz/450 ml)
Preparation 10 min
Cooking 25 min

— 4 tablespoons (2 oz/50 g)
  butter
— ¼ cup (1 oz/25 g) all-purpose
  (plain) flour
— 2 cups (16 fl oz/475 ml) milk
— pinch of freshly grated nutmeg
  (optional)
— salt and pepper

Melt the butter in a saucepan over medium heat. Remove the pan from the heat and whisk in the flour to make a smooth paste. Using a wooden spoon, gradually stir in all the milk, making sure the sauce is smooth between each addition.

Return the pan to the heat and cook over medium-high heat, stirring continuously until it starts to boil. Season with salt, lower the heat, cover, and simmer gently over low heat, stirring occasionally, for at least 20 minutes. The sauce should be thick enough to coat the

back of the spoon and not run off. Remove the pan from the heat. Season to taste, and add the nutmeg, if using.

Béchamel sauce should not taste floury. If the sauce is too thick, add a little more milk. If too runny, boil for a little longer. For a richer béchamel sauce, replace half the milk with the same amount of heavy (double) cream; for a lighter sauce, replace half the milk with the same amount of water.

Use in gratins or lasagne.

Red Pepper Sauce

Makes 1¼ cups (10 fl oz/300 ml)
Preparation 15 min, plus cooling
Cooking 10 min

— 2 large red bell peppers
— 2 tablespoons white wine
 vinegar
— 2 cloves garlic, chopped
— 3 tablespoons olive oil
— salt

Blanch the bell peppers in a saucepan of salted, boiling water for 5 minutes, then drain and leave to cool slightly. Peel off the skins, halve, and remove the seeds and membranes. Chop coarsely, then process in a food processor to a puree.

Pour the vinegar into the same saucepan, add the garlic, and heat for a few minutes. Strain the vinegar into the food processor and add the oil. Process until smooth.

Serve immediately with steamed fish or boiled meat.

Ragu

Makes 2 lb/900 g
Preparation 15 min
Cooking 25 min

— 3 tablespoons olive oil
— 1 carrot, chopped
— 1 onion, chopped
— 1 lb 2 oz/500 g ground meat
— ⅔ cup (5 fl oz/150 ml) dry
 white wine
— 1⅔ cup (14 oz/400 g) canned,
 pureed tomatoes (passata)
— salt and pepper

Heat the olive oil in a saucepan, add the carrot and onion, and cook over low heat, stirring occasionally, for 5 minutes.

Add the meat and cook until browned, then pour in the wine and cook until it has evaporated.

Season with salt, add the tomatoes, cover, and simmer for 15 minutes. Season with pepper.

Serve immediately with pasta or freeze for future use.

Sage Butter

Makes 3 fl oz/90 ml
Preparation 5 min
Cooking 10 min

— 7 tablespoons (3½ oz/100 g) butter
— 15 fresh sage leaves
— salt

Melt the butter in a small saucepan over low heat. As soon as it starts to color, add the sage leaves and season with salt. Cook over low heat for 8 minutes. Remove the pan from the heat.

Serve immediately with pasta, meat, or boiled rice.

Sweet Fritter Batter

Makes 1²⁄₃ cup (14 fl oz/400 ml)
Preparation 15 min

— 1¼ cups (5 oz/150 g) all-purpose (plain) flour
— 1 teaspoon baking powder
— 2 tablespoons superfine (caster) sugar
— 1 cup (9 fl oz/250 ml) whole (full-fat) milk
— 1 egg
— 1 teaspoon vanilla extract

Sift (sieve) the flour, baking powder, and sugar into a bowl. Beat together the milk, egg, and vanilla in a small bowl, then whisk this mixture gradually into the flour until you have a smooth batter.

Use to coat fruit for deep-frying.

Crêpes

Makes 12
Preparation 10 min
Cooking 20 min

— vegetable oil, for frying

For the crêpe batter
— 2 cups (9 oz/250 g) flour
— 2 eggs
— 2½ cups (1 pint/600 ml) milk
— 4 tablespoons (2 oz/50 g) butter, melted

To make the batter, sift (sieve) the flour into a mixing bowl. Beat the eggs and milk together in a small bowl and gradually beat into the flour, then stir in the melted butter. Freeze the batter for future use or use straightaway to make crêpes.

To make the crêpes, heat 1 teaspoon of oil in a skillet or frying pan until hot. Add a ladleful of the batter and swirl the skillet so that the batter covers the bottom of the skillet. Cook for 1 minute, or until golden underneath. Flip the crêpe and cook for another 30 seconds– 1 minute until golden underneath. Transfer to a plate. Repeat with the remaining batter, and stack them, separated with wax (greaseproof) paper, on a plate. Keep warm before serving.

Cooking Time Index

10 minutes

15 minutes

20 minutes

25 minutes

30 minutes

Index

H
hake in green sauce 117

ham
  Belgian endive with
    Prague ham 153
  ham and sage frittata 100
  penne alla vodka 76

herbs
  baby carrots in herb
    sauce 170
  frittata with aromatic
    herbs 105
  ten-herb sausages 148

J
jam tart 219

L
lasagne Bolognese 80
leeks, baked eggs
  with 108
lemon, tagliatelle with 64
lettuce and mint soup 97
liver, Veneto-style 147

M
Marsala
  veal scallops with
    Marsala 144
  zabaglione 196
mayonnaise 226
Milanese risotto 86
Milanese veal chops 142
mint: lettuce and mint
  soup 97
mushrooms
  mushroom risotto 85
  steak with mushrooms 136
  tortiglioni with mushroom
    and eggplant 50
mussels marinara 126

O
olives
  orange salad 186
  penne with black olives 56
  radish salad with olives 185
  rolled bell peppers 27
  tuna with almonds, pine
    nuts, and olives 114
oranges
  orange salad 186
  Treviso radicchio salad
    with orange 182

P
pancetta
  chicken roulades with
    sage 130
  linguine with broccoli and
    pancetta 74
  peas with pancetta 162
  red cabbage, pancetta, and
    Roquefort salad 180
panzanella 22
pasta
  conchiglie with Gorgonzola
    and pistachios 61
  conchiglie with
    mozzarella 38
  conchiglie with spinach 46
  fettuccine with chicken
    and almonds 73
  fettuccine with walnut
    sauce 58
  lasagne Bolognese 80
  linguine with broccoli and
    pancetta 74
  linguine with Genoese
    pesto 49
  macaroni au gratin 62
  orecchiette with
    broccoli 43

pappardelle with
  cauliflower and
  Gorgonzola 40
pasta with tomato sauce 32
penne arrabbiata 37
penne alla vodka 76
penne with black olives 56
pizza-style fusilli 34
rigatoni with garbanzo
  bean sauce 52
spaghetti carbonara 79
spaghetti with garlic and
  chili oil 67
spaghettini with clams 68
spring linguine 44
tagliatelle with lemon 64
tagliatelle with salmon 70
taglierini with shallots 55
tortiglioni with mushroom
  and eggplant 50

pears
  chocolate and pear
    tart 216
  pears in chocolate 207
peas
  peas with pancetta 162
  spring linguine 44
pesto, Genoese 49
pickled onions: summer
  rice salad 88
pine nuts: tuna with
  almonds, pine nuts,
  and olives 114
pistachios, conchiglie with
  Gorgonzola and 61
pizza-style fusilli 34
plums in wine 204

pomegranate, mixed salad
with 179
pork chops in butter and
sage 150
potatoes
garbanzo bean and
radicchio salad 176
linguine with Genoese
pesto 49
new potatoes with
rosemary 174
Prague ham, Belgian endive
with 153
prosciutto
Roman saltimbocca 141
tenderloin of beef with
fava beans 135

R
radicchio
garbanzo bean and
radicchio salad 176
Treviso radicchio salad
with orange 182
radishes
carpaccio 28
radish salad with
olives 185
ragu 80, 227
rice salad, summer 88
ricotta cheese: conchiglie
with spinach 46
risotto
asparagus risotto 82
Milanese risotto 86
mushroom risotto 85
Roman saltimbocca 141
rosemary
broiled salmon with
rosemary 112

new potatoes with
rosemary 174
roulades
chicken, anchovy, and
caper roulades 132
chicken roulades with
sage 130

S
sage
chicken roulades with
sage 130
ham and sage frittata 100
pork chops in butter and
sage 150
Roman saltimbocca 141
sage appetizers 10
sage butter 228
salads
buffalo milk mozzarella
Caprese salad 12
chicken and celeriac
salad 191
fennel, celery, and apple
salad 188
garbanzo bean and
radicchio salad 176
mixed salad with
pomegranate 179
orange salad 186
radish salad with
olives 185
red cabbage, pancetta,
and Roquefort salad 180
shrimp and corn salad 192
summer rice salad 88
Treviso radicchio salad
with orange 182
white bean and asparagus
salad 158

salmon
broiled salmon with
rosemary 112
tagliatelle with salmon 70
saltimbocca, Roman 141
sandwiches, fried
mozzarella 111
sauces
béchamel sauce 226
red pepper sauce 227
tomato sauce 32
sausages
sausage crostini 18
ten-herb sausages 148
scallions, braised 173
scallops, skewered sea 129
sea bass baked in a
package 118
shallots, taglierini with 55
shrimp
shrimp and corn salad 192
shrimp with almonds and
bread crumbs 124
skewered sea scallops 129
smoothies
strawberry smoothie 222
summer smoothie 220
sole
delicious sole 123
sole with thyme 120
soups
bread soup with tomato 94
cream of carrot soup 92
lettuce and mint soup 97
watercress soup 91
spinach, conchiglie with 46
spring linguine 44
strawberry smoothie 222
summer cannellini
beans 161
summer rice salad 88
summer smoothie 220

Phaidon Press Limited
Regent's Wharf
All Saints Street
London N1 9PA

Phaidon Press Inc.
65 Bleecker Street
New York, NY 10012

www.phaidon.com

© 2015 Phaidon Press Limited
ISBN 978 0 7148 7058 8

Quick and Easy Italian Recipes originates from:
Il cucchiaio d'argento, first published in 1950, eighth
edition (revised, expanded and redesigned) 1997;
Il cucchiaio d'argento Cucina Regionale, first
published in 2008; *Il cucchiaio d'argento estate*,
first published in 2005; *Primi piatti*, first published
2004; from *Second piatti*, first published 2005; and
from *Antipasti e contorni*, first published in 2007.
© Editoriale Domus S.p.A with the exception of
recipes on pages 219, bottom recipe 228, and
229, which were developed by Katy Greenwood.

A CIP catalogue record for this book is available from
the Library of Congress.

Commissioning Editor: Emilia Terragni
Project Editor: Elizabeth Clinton
Production Controller: Adela Cory
Design by atlas.
Photographs by Steven Joyce, Jason Lowe,
Edward Park, and Andy Sewell

Printed in Italy

The publishers would like to thank Jane Bamforth,
Theresa Bebbington, Vanessa Bird, Carmen Figini, Jan
Fullwood, Katy Greenwood, Michelle Lo, Ellie Smith,
Tara Stevens, Hans Stofregen, Gemma Wilson, and
Jade Zimmerman for their contributions to the book.

RECIPE NOTES

Butter should always be unsalted.

Unless othewise stated, all herbs are fresh and
parsley is flat-leaf parsley.

Pepper is always freshly ground black pepper,
unless otherwise specified.

Eggs, vegetables, and fruits are assumed to be
large size, unless otherwise specified.

Milk is always full-fat (whole), unless otherwise
specified.

Garlic cloves are assumed to be large; use two
if yours are small.

Ham means cooked ham, unless otherwise
specified.

Prosciutto refers exclusively to raw, dry-cured
ham, usually from Parma or San Daniele in
northern Italy.

Cooking and preparation times are for guidance
only, as individual ovens vary. If using a fan oven,
follow the manufacturer's instructions concerning
oven temperatures.

To test whether your deep-frying oil is hot
enough, add a cube of stale bread. If it browns
in thirty seconds, the temperature is 350–375°F/
180–190°C, about right for most frying. Exercise
caution when deep frying: add the food carefully
to avoid splashing, wear long sleeves, and never
leave the pan unattended.

Some recipes include raw or very lightly cooked
eggs. These should be avoided particularly by the
elderly, infants, pregnant women, convalescents,
and anyone with an impaired immune system.

All spoon measurements are level.
1 teaspoon = 5 ml; 1 tablespoon = 15 ml.
Australian standard tablespoons are 20 ml,
so Australian readers are advised to use
3 teaspoons in place of 1 tablespoon when
measuring small quantities.